D3.js By Example

Create attractive web-based data visualizations using the amazing JavaScript library D3.js

Michael Heydt

BIRMINGHAM - MUMBAI

D3.js By Example

First published: December 2015

Production reference: 1181215

Published by Packt Publishing Ltd.
Livery Place
35 Livery Street
Birmingham B3 2PB, UK.

ISBN 978-1-78528-008-5

www.packtpub.com

Credits

Author
Michael Heydt

Reviewers
Patrick Cason
Pablo Núñez Navarro
William Sankey

Commissioning Editor
Veena Pagare

Acquisition Editors
Harsha Bharwani
Hemal Desai

Content Development Editor
Merwyn D'souza

Technical Editor
Parag Topre

Copy Editor
Sonia Mathur

Project Coordinator
Nikhil Nair

Proofreader
Safis Editing

Indexer
Monica Ajmera Mehta

Graphics
Disha Haria

Production Coordinator
Conidon Miranda

Cover Work
Conidon Miranda

About the Author

Michael Heydt is an independent consultant, programmer, educator, and trainer. He has a passion for learning and sharing his knowledge of new technologies. Michael has worked in multiple industry verticals, including media, finance, energy, and healthcare. Over the last decade, he worked extensively with web, cloud, and mobile technologies and managed user experience, interface design, and data visualization for major consulting firms and their clients. Michael's current company, Seamless Thingies (www.seamlessthingies.tech), focuses on IoT development and connecting everything with everything.

He is the author of numerous articles, papers, and books, such as *Instant Lucene. NET*, *Learning Pandas*, and *Mastering Pandas for Finance*, all by Packt Publishing, on technology. Michael is also a common speaker at .NET user groups and various mobile, cloud, and IoT conferences and delivers webinars on advanced technologies. He can be reached through his website e-mails, mike@heydt.org and mike@ seamlessthingies.tech and on Twitter at @mikeheydt.

About the Reviewers

Patrick Cason is a web developer and designer based in Nashville, Tennessee. He has experience working primarily as a front-end engineer, but he also dabbles in UI design and mobile development. Patrick started a few businesses in the past, but he currently tends to his latest endeavor, Octovis, as the lead front-end engineer and designer. He has worked on multiple data visualization projects in the American political domain, including both Change Politics and Poliana.

Pablo Núñez Navarro has written line of business applications for more than 15 years, from VB 6 to .NET and JavaScript among many other technologies. His work on long-live projects and software maintenance made him focus on best practices and clean code, with an intensive use of code reviewing to achieve consistency and readability through working in teams. Pablo enjoys discussing software.

He has taught many courses, including the University of Malaga's master's in RIAtec, for quite a few years. Pablo coauthored *Mastering LOB Development for Silverlight 5: a Case Study in Action*, *Packt Publishing*. He is also very active in local software communities.

My three wonderful kids, Julia, Marcos, and Claudia are a distraction and at the same time, a source of motivation for my work.

William Sankey is a data professional and developer hobbyist living in College Park, Maryland. He graduated in 2012 from Johns Hopkins University with a master's degree in public policy and specializes in quantitative analyses. He has worked in the public and private spheres and is currently a data scientist at Xometry.

I would like to thank my devoted wife, Julia, and rambunctious puppy, Ruby, for all their love and support.

www.PacktPub.com

Support files, eBooks, discount offers, and more

For support files and downloads related to your book, please visit www.PacktPub.com.

Did you know that Packt offers eBook versions of every book published, with PDF and ePub files available? You can upgrade to the eBook version at www.PacktPub.com and as a print book customer, you are entitled to a discount on the eBook copy. Get in touch with us at service@packtpub.com for more details.

At www.PacktPub.com, you can also read a collection of free technical articles, sign up for a range of free newsletters and receive exclusive discounts and offers on Packt books and eBooks.

https://www2.packtpub.com/books/subscription/packtlib

Do you need instant solutions to your IT questions? PacktLib is Packt's online digital book library. Here, you can search, access, and read Packt's entire library of books.

Why subscribe?

- Fully searchable across every book published by Packt
- Copy and paste, print, and bookmark content
- On demand and accessible via a web browser

Free access for Packt account holders

If you have an account with Packt at www.PacktPub.com, you can use this to access PacktLib today and view 9 entirely free books. Simply use your login credentials for immediate access.

Table of Contents

Preface

Learning D3.js on your own can be a daunting task. There are literally thousands of examples online with differing degrees of effective, or ineffective, explanation.

This book uses examples that take you right from the beginning, with the basic concepts of D3.js, using practical examples that progressively build on each other both within a specific chapter and also with reference to previous chapters.

We will focus on the examples created for this book as well as those found online that are excellent but could use some additional explanation. Each example will explain how the example works either line by line or by comparison with other examples and concepts learned earlier in the book.

What this book covers

Chapter 1, Getting Started with D3.js, introduces you to D3.js and building a simple application using several tools to help with its creation.

Chapter 2, Selections and Data Binding, teaches you how to use D3.js selections to create DOM elements based on data.

Chapter 3, Creating Visuals with SVG, introduces you to Scalable Vector Graphics and how to use them to render various shapes that are commonly used in D3.js visualizations.

Chapter 4, Creating a Bar Graph, demonstrates how to create a bar graph from given data.

Chapter 5, Using Data and Scales, shows you how to load data from external sources in different formats and convert it into information suitable for visualization.

Chapter 6, Creating Scatter and Bubble Plots, demonstrates how to load, scale, and plot multidimensional data in a manner that makes patterns clear to users.

Chapter 7, Creating Animated Visuals, teaches you to use animations in your D3.js applications to demonstrate how data changes over time.

Chapter 8, Adding User Interactivity, shows you how to allow users to interact with your visualizations using the mouse.

Chapter 9, Complex Shapes Using Paths, shows you how to use many of the built-in tools in D3.js to automatically generate complex paths with a few simple statements.

Chapter 10, Using Layouts to Visualize Series and Hierarchical Data, focuses on creating complex graphs that utilize the layout objects of D3.js. This includes a multitude of graphs in different categories, including stacked, packed, clustered, flow-based, hierarchical, and radial.

Chapter 11, Visualizing Information Networks, dives into demonstrating how you can use D3.js to visualize network data such as is found in social networks.

Chapter 12, Creating Maps with GeoJSON and TopoJSON, teaches you how to create maps and highlight regions on them using two forms of geographic data: Geo and TopoJSON.

Chapter 13, Combining D3.js and AngularJS, discusses how you can integrate multiple D3.js visualizations using Angular.js to create reactive visualizations.

What you need for this book

All of the tools used in this book are available on the Internet free of charge. All that is required is a modern web browser to run the samples, and all code can be edited and run online within the browser. To be specific about what makes up a modern browser, this includes Firefox, Chrome, Safari, Opera, IE9+, Android, and iOS.

Who this book is for

Whether you are new to data and data visualization, a seasoned data scientist, or a computer graphics specialist, this book will provide you with the skills you need to create web-based and interactive data visualizations. This book assumes some knowledge of coding and, in particular, experience in coding with JavaScript.

Conventions

In this book, you will find a number of text styles that distinguish between different kinds of information. Here are some examples of these styles and an explanation of their meaning.

Code words in text, database table names, folder names, filenames, file extensions, pathnames, dummy URLs, user input, and Twitter handles are shown as follows: "Now using the selector variable we call the .enter() function and assign it to a variable named entering."

A block of code is set as follows:

```
<div id='div1'>A</div>
<div id='div2'>B</div>
<div id='div3'>C</div>
<div id='div4'>D</div>
<script>
    var selector = d3.select('body')
                        .selectAll('div');
</script>
```

When we wish to draw your attention to a particular part of a code block, the relevant lines or items are set in bold:

```
function render(dataToRender) {
    var selector = d3.select('body')
        .selectAll('div')
        .data(dataToRender);

    var entering = selector.enter();
    entering.append('div')
        .text(function(d) { return d; });
}
```

New terms and **important words** are shown in bold. Words that you see on the screen, for example, in menus or dialog boxes, appear in the text like this: "The value for **Mikael** was changed to **25.**"

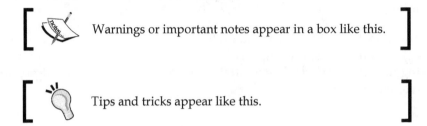

Warnings or important notes appear in a box like this.

Tips and tricks appear like this.

Reader feedback

Feedback from our readers is always welcome. Let us know what you think about this book—what you liked or disliked. Reader feedback is important for us as it helps us develop titles that you will really get the most out of.

To send us general feedback, simply e-mail feedback@packtpub.com, and mention the book's title in the subject of your message.

If there is a topic that you have expertise in and you are interested in either writing or contributing to a book, see our author guide at www.packtpub.com/authors.

Customer support

Now that you are the proud owner of a Packt book, we have a number of things to help you to get the most from your purchase.

Downloading the example code

All examples in this text are available to review, execute, and edit online. Reference to code are referred to as a **bl.ock** and be referenced as follows:

bl.ock (2.13): http://bl.ocks.org/d3byex/35641fbe385e5a162b84

This will take you to a page on http://bl.ocks.org/ for the example. This page will also contain a link to take you to jsbin.com where you can interactively make changes to the code.

You can download the example code files from your account at `http://www.packtpub.com` for all the Packt Publishing books you have purchased. If you purchased this book elsewhere, you can visit `http://www.packtpub.com/support` and `register` to have the files e-mailed directly to you.

Errata

Although we have taken every care to ensure the accuracy of our content, mistakes do happen. If you find a mistake in one of our books — maybe a mistake in the text or the code — we would be grateful if you could report this to us. By doing so, you can save other readers from frustration and help us improve subsequent versions of this book. If you find any errata, please report them by visiting `http://www.packtpub.com/submit-errata`, selecting your book, clicking on the **Errata Submission Form** link, and entering the details of your errata. Once your errata are verified, your submission will be accepted and the errata will be uploaded to our website or added to any list of existing errata under the Errata section of that title.

To view the previously submitted errata, go to `https://www.packtpub.com/books/content/support` and enter the name of the book in the search field. The required information will appear under the **Errata** section.

Piracy

Piracy of copyrighted material on the Internet is an ongoing problem across all media. At Packt, we take the protection of our copyright and licenses very seriously. If you come across any illegal copies of our works in any form on the Internet, please provide us with the location address or website name immediately so that we can pursue a remedy.

Please contact us at `copyright@packtpub.com` with a link to the suspected pirated material.

We appreciate your help in protecting our authors and our ability to bring you valuable content.

Questions

If you have a problem with any aspect of this book, you can contact us at `questions@packtpub.com`, and we will do our best to address the problem.

1
Getting Started with D3.js

D3.js is an open source JavaScript library that provides the facility for manipulating HTML documents based upon data, using JavaScript as the language for implementing the mapping of data to the documents. Hence, the name **D3 (Data Driven Documents)**. Many consider D3.js as a data visualization library. This may be correct, but D3.JS provides much more to its user than just visualization, such as:

- Efficient selection of items in the HTML DOM.
- Binding of data to visual elements.
- Specifications on handling the addition and removal of data items.
- The ability to style DOM elements dynamically.
- Definition of an interaction model for the user with the data.
- The ability to specify transitions between data visualizations based upon dynamic changes in data.
- D3.js helps you bring data to life using **HTML, SVG,** and **CSS**. It focuses on the data, the way it is presented to the user, the changes in visualization with changes in data, and the way the user interacts with data through the visualization.

We are about to start on a fabulous journey of discovery with creating rich data visualizations with D3.js, and focusing on project-based learning of D3.js through practical examples. We will start out with the basic concepts, and then move through various examples of creating living data visualizations with D3.js.

In this first chapter, we will start with a brief overview of several of the concepts in D3.js, create a minimal D3.js application, and examine several of the tools that you can use to build D3.js applications.

Specifically, in this chapter, we will cover the following topics:

- A brief overview of D3.js
- The key design features of D3.js, including selection, data management, interaction, animation, and modules
- An introduction to development tools to get you going quickly with D3.js
- A simple Hello World program using D3.js
- Examining the DOM generated by D3.js with the Google Chrome Developer tools

A brief overview of D3.js

D3.js is a JavaScript library for manipulating DOM objects based upon data. By using D3.js and modern browsers, specifically those which can display and manipulate SVG, you can create rich visualizations of data. These visualizations not only visualize the data, but can also include descriptions to change what is shown to the user based upon the changes in the data, and the way in which the user can interact with the visuals which represent the data.

 You can get D3.js at `http://d3js.org`.

D3 Data-Driven Documents

D3.js differs from other data visualization frameworks such as **Processing** (https://processing.org/) in that it provides a domain-specific language for transforming the DOM based upon data, whereas tools like Processing provide a lower level direct rendering model. D3.js lets you describe the means of visualizing the data instead of coding all of the specific details to draw the pixels of the visualizations. This facilitates easy creation of visualizations by allowing D3.js to worry about the details on rendering the data, based on the standards of SVG and CSS.

A fundamental concept in D3.js is the ability to easily manipulate the DOM in a web document. This is often a complicated problem, and many frameworks (such as **jQuery**) have been created to perform this task. D3.js provides capabilities similar to jQuery, and for those familiar with jQuery, much of D3.js will feel familiar.

But D3.js takes what libraries like jQuery provide and extends them to provide a more declarative nature of modifying the DOM to create visuals based on the structure of the data instead of simply being a framework for low level DOM manipulation.

This is important, as data visualization requires more than an ability to simply modify the DOM; it should also describe how the DOM should be changed when data is modified, including the way it changes when the user interacts with the visual elements representing the data.

 We will not cover jQuery in this book. Our focus will purely be on how we can manipulate the DOM using the facilities provided by D3.js. We will use D3.js constructs to apply styles instead of depending on CSS. All of this is to exemplify how to use the facilities of D3.js instead of hiding any of it with other tools.

We will examine many concepts in D3.js in detail, but let's start with a few high-level ideas in D3.js that are worth mentioning first.

Selections

The core operation in D3.js is **selection**, which is a filtered set of DOM elements queried from the document. As the data changes (that is, it is either loaded or modified), the result of the selection filter is changed by D3.js based on how the data was changed. Hence, the visual representation also changes.

D3.js uses the W3C selectors API (http://www.w3.org/TR/selectors-api/) for identifying the items in the DOM. This is a mini-language consisting of predicates that can filter the elements in the DOM by tag, class, id, attribute, containment, adjacency, and several other facets of the DOM. Predicates can also be intersected or unioned, resulting in a rich and concise selection of elements.

Selections are implemented by D3.js through the global namespace d3, which provides the d3.select() and d3.selectAll() functions. These functions utilize the mini-language and return, respectively, the first or all items matching the specification. Using the result of these selections, D3.js provides additional abilities for modifying those elements based upon your data using a process known as **data binding**.

Data and data binding

The data in D3.js is **bound** to the DOM elements. Through **binding**, D3.js tracks a collection of objects along with their properties, and based upon rules that you specify, it modifies the DOM of the document based upon that data. This binding is performed through various operators provided by D3.js, which can easily be used to describe the mapping of the visual representation of the data. At this point, we'll introduce the three stages of data binding, and dive into more details on the process in *Chapter 2, Selections and Data Binding*.

The process of binding in D3.js consists of three stages: **Enter**, **Update**, and **Exit**. When performing a selection for the first time with D3.js, you can specify the data that is to be bound and needs to be entered. You can also specify the code to be executed for each of these stages.

When data is first joined into a selection, new visuals will need to be created in the DOM for each data item. This is performed using the enter process which is started by calling the .enter() function. Code that you specify after the .enter() function will be used to specify each and every piece of data that is represented visually, and D3.js will use this code to automatically generate the DOM that is required instead of you needing to code it all in detail.

As the application modifies this bound data, we will execute the selection repeatedly. D3.js will make a note of the existing visuals and the data they are bound to, and allow us to make modifications to the visuals based upon the way the data changed.

If data items are removed, we can use the D3.js .exit() function in a selection to inform D3.js to remove the visuals from the display. Normally, this is done by telling D3.js to remove the associated DOM elements, but we can also execute animations to make the removal demonstrate to the user how the visual is changing instead of a jarring change of display.

If we create a selection without an explicit reference to .enter() or .exit(), we are informing D3.js that we want to potentially make modifications to the visuals that are already bound to the data. This gives us the chance to examine the properties of each data item and instruct D3.js on changing the bound visuals appropriately.

This separation of enter, update, and exit processes allows for very precise control of the visual element lifecycle. These states allow you to update visuals as the data changes either internally or through user interaction. It also gives you the ability to provide well-defined transitions or animations for each of the three states, which are essential for dynamic data visualizations that demonstrate data not simply statically but also how it changes through motion.

Interaction and animation

D3.js provides facilities for animating the visual elements based upon the changes in data or upon events created by the user such as mouse events. These are performed by integrating with the events in the DOM using the .on() function as part of a selection.

D3.js event handlers are similar to those provided by jQuery. However, instead of just calling a function, they also expose the bound data item to the function, and if you want, the index of the data item in a collection. This saves us from having to write code that looks up the data item based upon things like mouse positions, and therefore, greatly simplifies our code.

Additionally, through integration with the enter, update, and exit selection processes, we can declaratively code scene transitions in each of these scenarios. These transitions expose the style and attr operators of the selections. Any changes that we make to those properties are noticed by D3.js, which will then apply an **interpolator** to transition the property values from the previous to the new values over a given period of time.

By using interpolation, we can avoid coding the repeated changes in the values of the visual properties (such as location and color) at each step of the animation. D3.js does all this for us automatically!

Additionally, D3.js automatically manages the scheduling of animations and transitions. This removes the need for you to manage complicated concurrency issues and guarantees exclusive access to the resources for each element along with highly optimized animation through a shared timer managed by D3.js.

Modules

D3.js provides a number of **modules** of prebuilt functionality for helping us code many of the things that we need to do for creating rich and interactive data visualizations. These modules in D3.js are grouped into a number of generated categories based upon the capabilities provided to the programmer.

- **Shapes**: The shapes module gives us numerous prebuilt visuals including, and not limited to, lines, arcs, areas, and scatterplot symbols. By using D3.js shapes, we can simply add the geometric renderings to the visualization, and not worry about drawing each in detail, pixel by pixel.

- **Scales**: This module gives us a means of converting data values into coordinates within the browser. These save us from coding repetitive, complex, and often error-prone translations by providing them out of the box. They also provide the basis for generating the visuals for axes, again saving us much effort in rendering visuals that would otherwise be complicated.

- **Layouts**: The layouts module gives us the tools to easily (if not automatically) calculate the visual relationships between the elements in our visualizations. This is often the most complicated part of data visualizations, and D3.js provides us with many prebuilt hierarchical and physical layouts that make our lives as programmers much simpler.

- **Behaviors**: This module provides implementations of the common user interaction patterns. An example would be a selection behavior that implements listening to the mouse events on visual elements, and changes the presentation of the item to represent that the user has selected it.

- **Data-processing modules**: D3.js also includes various data-processing utilities such as nest and cross operators, and parsers for data in formats, such as CSV, JSON, TSV, and for data, in date and number formats.

We will discuss these modules in detail in their dedicated chapters.

Tools for creating and sharing D3.js visualizations

D3.js applications can be built using many, if not any, web development tools. The choice of tool is often dependent upon the individual coder, as each platform (.Net, Node.JS, Ruby on Rails, and so on) provides their own (and many third-party) tools.

This book will not be prescriptive and specify editors. Instead, it will generally refer you to the online and functional examples of all the code, and leave it to the readers to reproduce them in their own development environment.

The examples in this book will be delivered using a combination of **Js Bin** (http:// jsbin.com/) and **bl.ocks.org** (http://bl.ocks.org/), and we will use the Google Chrome Developer tools for examining the DOM in our examples. A brief introduction to each is therefore worthwhile, as each example in this book will be linked to an example on bl.ocks.org, which itself will contain a link to the code in Js Bin for you to play with dynamically.

Js Bin

Js Bin (http://jsbin.com/) is a website that functions as a development tool for facilitating the quick creation and sharing of simple JavaScript applications that run within the browser. It provides many features, including saving and sharing of HTML and JavaScript, real-time update of the UI while you are editing, and a very cool ability to push your code and data to GitHub.

 GitHub is a free code sharing and source code management tool. If you are not familiar with it, check it out at http://www.github.com.

I think that Js Bin provides one of the least-friction means of getting up and coding with D3.js. You can simply go to the website, start editing in HTML, CSS, or JavaScript, and see the results as you type in the browser pane. No need for installing any development tools or web servers!

As an example of Js Bin, the following link will take you to the first of our examples, the canonical Hello World application written purely in HTML. `http://jsbin.com/zimeqe/edit?html,output`.

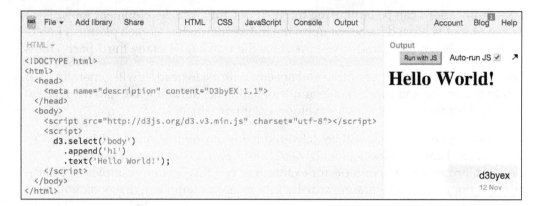

 Don't worry right now about the code embedded in HTML in this demonstration. We will again look at this example along with more complicated ones later in this chapter.

The preceding screenshot displays a single bin, a combination of HTML, CSS, and JavaScript that is stored within Js Bin's servers. The Js Bin user interface provides multiple tabs/panes for the HTML, CSS, JavaScript, Console, and HTML output from the code in the bin. With **Auto-run JS** selected, the output will be regenerated on every interactive change to any of the code.

This makes Js Bin excellent for interactively demonstrating and creating D3.js visualizations.

bl.ocks.org

bl.ocks.org (`http://bl.ocks.org`) is a service for D3.js code examples that you place on GitHub, a free source code and sharing repository, in an entity known as a gist. A gist is simply one or more reusable and sharable piece of code that are managed by GitHub. They are an excellent means of remembering and sharing small code examples.

bl.ocks.org was created by Mike Bostock, the original creator of D3.js. It is able to create great D3.js visualizations using gists, provided that the gist itself is a piece of D3.js code. Many, if not most, D3.js examples on the Web are presented as examples on bl.ocks.org, and this book will follow this model.

For a demonstration, open `http://bl.ocks.org/d3byex/ed79b9fee311091333d6`, which takes you to a bl.ock.org version of the **Hello World** example. Opening the link will present you with the following content.

This bl.ock follows a pattern that will be used throughout the book. Each example will be in its own bl.ocks.org and consist of a title, the D3.js code in operation, a link to live code on Js Bin, and then the HTML and any data that is in use in the example.

At the very top of the page, there is a link that you can click which will also take you to the gist on GitHub.

The link displayed in the preceding screenshot takes you to the following page at `https://gist.github.com/d3byex/ed79b9fee311091333d6`

This code is not dynamic like the one on Js Bin, but you can click on the **Download Zip** button, and all the files in the gist get downloaded to your system as a ZIP file.

Google Chrome and Developer tools

D3.js applications can be developed in any number of tools. In this book, we will use Google Chrome as a browser, and use its embedded development tools. You can also use Firefox or Internet Explorer and their respective development plugins. Theoretically, all the examples will run identically in all three browsers, but have only been tested in Google Chrome.

You can access the developer tools from the Chrome settings button, or by using the key combination of *option + command + I* (on Mac) or *Ctrl + Shift + I* (on Windows). Pressing the *F12* button also takes you to the Chrome Developer tools on a Windows platform.

The following screenshot demonstrates the Google Chrome Developer tools open on the **Epicyclic Gearing** bl.ock at `http://bl.ocks.org/mbostock/1353700`

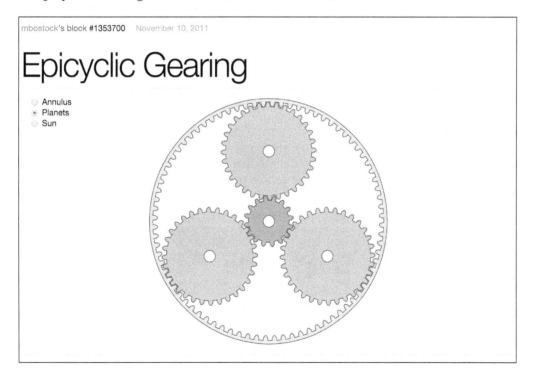

On opening the developer tools, you will be presented with a panel that opens in the browser which displays the details of the content on the page.

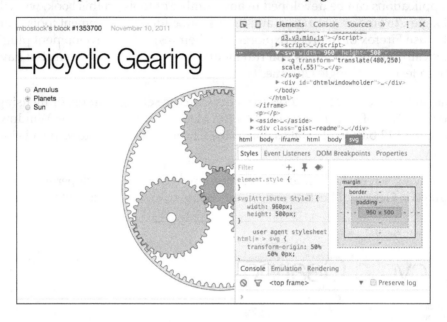

In this case the pane opens on the right (you can configure the location where it opens), and displays the HTML for the page with the main SVG element of the page highlighted. While selecting nodes in HTML, the tools will highlight that element in the web page, and display the selected details for the element, in this case, the styles. We will use these tools in *Chapter 2*, *Selections and Data Binding*, to demonstrate how D3.js binds data to the DOM elements, and in later chapters to understand how.

Hello World – D3.js style

Now let's apply what we have learned in this chapter by stepping through an example, and see how we use D3.js to modify the DOM. The example will be the same as the one we just saw in the previous section; we'll walk through it to see how it functions.

The following is the entire entire HTML for the application:

```
<!DOCTYPE html>
<html>
  <head>
    <meta name="description" content="D3byEX 1.1>
  </head>
  <body>
```

```
<script src="http://d3js.org/d3.v3.min.js"
        charset="utf-8"></script>
<script>
  d3.select('body')
    .append('h1')
    .text('Hello World!');
</script>
  </body>
</html>
```

bl.ock (1.1): `http://goo.gl/7KkIuC`

The code appends a level one header using an h1 tag to the body tag of the document. The h1 tag then has its content set to the text Hello World. And as we saw earlier, the output in the browser looks like the following screenshot:

Hello World!

There are two primary parts to this application, both of which we will see in almost every example. The first part includes a reference to the D3.js script, which is performed with the following code placed just inside the <body> tag:

```
<script src="http://d3js.org/d3.v3.min.js"
        charset="utf-8"></script>
```

This references the minified D3.js file directly from the D3.js (`http://d3js.org/`) website. You can also copy this file and place it locally on your web server or in a Web project. Since all the examples in this book are online, we will always use this URL.

Note that we also have to specify charset="utf-8". This is normally not required for most JavaScript libraries, but D3.js is UTF-8 encoded and not including this can cause issues. So, make sure you don't forget this attribute.

The actual D3.js code in this example consists of the following three functions placed within another <script> tag within the body of the document.

```
d3.select('body')
  .append('h1')
  .text('Hello World!');
```

Let's examine how this puts the text in the web page.

```
d3.select('body')
```

All D3.js statements will start with the use of the `d3` namespace. This is the root of where we start accessing all the D3.js functions. In this line, we call the `.select()` function, passing its `body`. This is telling D3.js to find the first body element in the document and return it to us for performing other operations upon it.

The `.select()` function returns a D3.js object representing the body DOM object. We can immediately call `.append('h1')` to add the header element inside the body of the document.

The `.append()` function returns another D3.js object, but this one represents the new `h1` DOM element. So all we need to do is to make a **chained** call: `.text('Hello World!')`, and our code is complete.

This process of calling functions in this manner is referred to in D3.js parlance as **chaining,** and in general, it is referred to as a **fluent** API in programming languages. This chaining is the aforementioned mini-language. Each chained D3.js function call further specifies the operation, allowing you to very easily describe how you want to modify the DOM through chained method calls.

This sometimes feels strange to those who have not had experience in using a fluent syntax, but once you get used to it, I guarantee that you will see the reason behind using this type of syntax. As we will see through the examples that we cover, this provides us with a very concise means of declaratively instructing D3.js on what we want in our visualization.

For those familiar with jQuery, this syntax will look familiar. An equivalent piece of code could be written in JQuery as `$('body').append('h1').text('Hello World');`

But as we will see in more complex examples, the features provided by D3.js will give us much more power to create data visualizations than can be done with jQuery.

Examining the DOM generated by D3.js

Now let's take a quick look at the DOM that was created by this code using the Chrome Developer Tools. Open the developer tools using the instructions given earlier in the chapter. I prefer mine to be displayed to the right of the page, and the book will follow this convention.

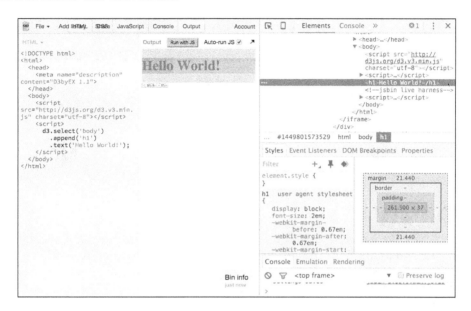

Since this example (and all the examples in this book) is hosted within Js Bin, there is a bunch of HTML content generated automatically and injected into our page by the backend of Js Bin. To find the element corresponding to the text generated by our code, you can drill through the DOM in the explorer. Otherwise, you can right-click on the element in the output pane of the browser, and select **Inspect Element** as seen in the following screenshot:

Then you can move directly to the element in the developer tools.

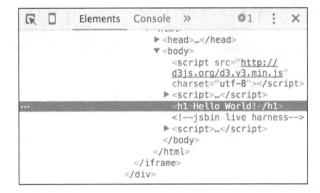

In the preceding screenshot, we can visually verify that the `<body>` tag had a new `<h1>` tag added with the text as we desired.

Summary

In this chapter, we looked at several high level concepts in D3.js: selections, data, interactions and animation, and modules. Then we briefly covered several of the tools that can be used to build D3.js applications, and which will be used in examples that follow in the remainder the book: Js Bin, bl.ocks.org, Google Chrome, and Google Chrome Developer tools. We closed the chapter with a very simple example that demonstrates how to include D3.js in your application and performing a simple selection that inserts content into the web page.

In the next chapter, we will expand upon the concept of selection and use it to bind data to visual elements in the DOM. We will expand our use of D3.js to create and modify DIV elements. Further on in *Chapter 3, Creating Visuals with SVG*, we will get into the real power of D3.js by using it to manipulate SVG.

2
Selections and Data Binding

In this chapter, you will learn how to use D3.js to select and manipulate the DOM of an HTML page based upon data. Rendering of visuals in D3.js takes a declarative approach, where you inform D3.js of how to visualize a piece of data instead of imperatively programming exactly how to draw the visual and iterate across the data. This process is referred to as **selection** and **data binding** in the D3.js nomenclature.

To demonstrate how D3.js can be used to create DOM elements driven by data, we will progress through a number of examples that demonstrate creating DIV elements to display various arrays of integer values. We will first examine how selection can be used to extract the existing DOM elements, and how D3.js is used to associate the data to each DOM element. Then we will examine the ways to instruct D3.js to create new DOM elements from the data. That will be followed by discussing the procedure for updating the existing elements, and for removing visual elements when particular data items are removed.

We will focus purely upon the HTML DOM elements, and will progress to using SVG in later chapters. Specifically, we will progress through the following topics in this chapter:

- Using D3.js selections to modify DOM elements
- Modifying the style of DOM elements using D3.js selectors
- Binding data to the DOM using `.data()`
- Using `.enter()` for creating DOM elements from new data items
- Updating the existing DOM elements based upon the changes in data
- Using `.exit()` to remove DOM elements when the associated data is no longer to be visualized
- A laundry list of tips on performing data binding with D3.js

D3.js selections

At its core, D3.js is about selection, which is a process of finding and creating DOM elements that visualize data. At a simple level, a selection can just be a means of finding and manipulating elements in the DOM that already exist. However, D3.js selections can also be used for explicitly creating new elements in the DOM as well as for implicitly creating and removing DOM elements based upon the changes in an underlying data model.

In *Chapter 1, Getting Started with D3.js*, we saw a simple example of selection in which we used selection to make a D3.js version of the canonical Hello World application. Now we will dive deeper into the power of selections. We will look at two examples of selecting a DOM element and changing its style.

Changing the style of a DOM element

In this first example, we will create a page with four `div` elements, each with a unique ID. We will then use D3.js to find the first `div` tag, and change its background color.

bl.ock (2.1): `http://goo.gl/EnAQBc`

The `body` tag of the document contains the following code:

```
<div id='div1'>A</div>
<div id='div2'>B</div>
<div id='div3'>C</div>
<div id='div4'>D</div>
<script>
  d3.select('div').style('background-color', 'lightblue')
</script>
```

The result of this preceding code is as follows:

```
A
B
C
D
```

This example uses the d3.select() function, which returns the first element in the DOM that matches the given tag — in this case, 'DIV'. The result of d3.select() is a D3.js object representing the DOM element that was identified and the data that D3.js has associated with that element.

This concept in D3.js is referred to as a **selector**. The function d3.select() always represents a single DOM element or a null value if the element is not found.

A selector has methods such as .style(), which can be used to change the CSS style properties of the underlying element, attributes using .attr(), and the text property using the .text() function.

In this case, we use the .style() function to set the background-color property of the DIV elements style to lightblue.

Changing the style of multiple items

To select multiple items in the DOM, we can use the d3.selectAll() function. The result is a selector which can represent multiple DOM elements that match the criteria.

To demonstrate, we will change the single line of the D3.js code in our previous example to the following:

```
d3.selectAll('div').style('background-color', 'lightblue')
```

As a result of this, the call to .selectAll() will represent each of the four div elements in the document. The call to .style() will be applied to each of the DOM element represented, which results in the following output:

bl.ock (2.2): http://goo.gl/61p8Nv

This demonstrates one of the advantages of using D3.js for selection. Chained function calls will be applied to all DOM elements resulting from a D3.js selection. Therefore, we do not need to explicitly iterate through all the items. This saves us from excessive coding, and helps in reducing the potential of errors.

 Note that, by default, the items in a selector are fixed at the time of the creation of the D3.js selector. If we were to add another `div` after the selection, then the elements in the existing selector will not have the new `div` tag added.

The parameter passed to the functions `d3.select()` and `d3.selectAll()` can also include various CSS rules as part of the query. As an example, to select all the elements with a specific ID, prepend the parameter with #. The following example selects only those DOM elements whose id is `div2`:

```
d3.selectAll('#div2').style('background-color', 'lightblue')
```

This results in the following output:

 bl.ock (2.3): `http://goo.gl/TC4Yox`

Note that this selection will return all the DOM elements which have the ID `div2`, be they `div` or other types of DOM elements. This example only has `div` tags, so that is all that we will retrieve. Moreover, it is bad practice to have identical ID values on a page. But the way in which the query functions is viable.

If we want to ensure that this query returns only `div` elements, then we can use the following query, which places the type of the element before the hash symbol:

```
d3.selectAll("div#div3").style('background-color', 'lightblue')
```

The preceding query has the following result:

```
A
B
C
D
```

bl.ock (2.4): `http://goo.gl/xVwV10`

Now let's examine the scenario where we would like to apply a different style to each DOM element in the selector. To do this, we can pass an accessor function to the `.style()` instead of a value. For example, the following code will alternate the color of the background of the `div` tags between `lightblue` and `lightgray`.

```
d3.selectAll("div")
    .style('background-color', function (d, i) {
        return (i % 2 === 0) ? "lightblue" : "lightgray";
    });
```

The preceding code results in the following output:

```
A
B
C
D
```

bl.ock (2.5): `http://goo.gl/PdohHx`

Accessor functions are commonly used through D3.js. An accessor function has two parameters, the first of which represents the datum that has been associated by D3.js to the DOM element (we'll come back to this later in the chapter). The second parameter represents the 0-based array position of the DOM element in the result of the selection.

The second parameter of an accessor function is optional.

The return value of the selector function is another selector (or the same selector) in many cases. This allows us to chain the method calls together. We can do this to conveniently set multiple styles on all the DOM elements represented by the selector.

As an example, the following code first sets the background color, and then sets the width of each DIV to an increasing value:

```
d3.selectAll("div")
  .style('width', function(d, i) {
    return (10 + 10 * i) + "px";
  })
  .style('background-color', function (d, i) {
    return (i % 2 === 0) ? 'lightblue' : 'lightgray';
  });
```

The output for the preceding code will be as follows:

 bl.ock (2.6): `http://goo.gl/ukFFYL`

Multiple style properties can also be set in a single call to `.style()` by passing a hash of property names and values. The following has the same result as the previous example:

```
d3.selectAll("div").style({
    width: function (d, i) { return (10 + 10 * i) + "px" },
    'background-color': function (d, i) {
        return (i % 2 === 0) ? 'lightblue' : 'lightgray';
    }
});
```

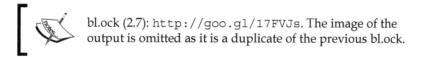

bl.ock (2.7): `http://goo.gl/17FVJs`. The image of the output is omitted as it is a duplicate of the previous bl.ock.

D3.js and data binding

The example in the previous section relied upon the elements that already exist in the DOM. Normally, in D3.js we would start with a set of data, and then build visualizations based on this data. We would also want to change the visualization as the data changes as a result of either adding more data items, removing some or all of them, or changing the properties of the existing objects.

This process of managing mapping of data to visual elements is often referred to as **binding of data**, and in terms of the D3.js nomenclature, it is referred to as a **data join** (do not confuse this with an SQL join). Binding in D3.js is performed by using the `.data()` function of a selector.

Let's dive in, and examine a few examples of binding data in some detail.

Data binding

Binding of data can be one of the hardest things for someone new to D3.js to get used to. Even for somebody who uses other languages and frameworks that provide data binding, the way in which D3.js binds data is a little different, and getting to know how it does so will save a lot of time down the road. Therefore, we will take the time to examine it in detail as it is essential for creating effective D3.js visualizations.

In D3.js, we drive the visualization of data through binding using the following functions of a selector.

Function	Purpose
`.data()`	Specifies the data to be used to drive the visualization
`.enter()`	Returns a selector representing the new items to be displayed
`.exit()`	Returns a selector representing the items that are no longer to be displayed

This pattern in which test functions are used is so ingrained in the D3.js code that it is often referred to as the **enter/update/exit** pattern or **general update** pattern. It provides a powerful means of declaratively telling D3.js how you want the dynamic data to be displayed, and to let D3.js handle the rendering.

We will come back to these details of the specifics of enter/update/exit in a little bit. For now, let's start by examining our selection example from earlier in the chapter, where we selected all the `div` objects in the document. This will help us understand the basis of how a selector facilitates the rendering process.

We will use a slight variant on the `d3.selectAll()` function from the previous example. Here, we will assign the result to a variable named `selector`:

```
<div id='div1'>A</div>
<div id='div2'>B</div>
<div id='div3'>C</div>
<div id='div4'>D</div>
<script>
    var selector = d3.select('body')
                        .selectAll('div');
</script>
```

bl.ock (2.8): `http://goo.gl/etDgJV`. The output is not shown as the code does give results visually different from the previous examples.

There are two other subtle differences in this preceding statement from the previous examples. The first is that we select the body DOM element, and the second is that we chain a call to `.selectAll()` for the div tags.

Using this pattern of a function chain, we are instructing D3.js to select all the `div` tags that are a child of the `body` tag. This chaining of select function calls allows us to navigate through the HTML document to look for tags in specific places, and as we will see shortly, specify where to put the new visual elements.

To help conceptualize a selector, I believe that a selector can be thought of as a collection of mappings between the DOM elements and the data that D3.js has associated with those element(s). I find it useful to mentally picture a selector with diagrams such as the following:

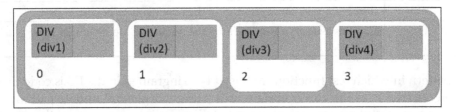

The orange part in the preceding diagram represents the overall selector that results from our selection. This selector contains four items represented by white, rounded rectangles, one for each div, and which we can think of as being numbered from 0 through 3.

Do not confuse a selector with an array – the individual elements in this diagram cannot be accessed using [].

The ordering is important as we will see when we update the data. By default, the ordering depends on how the identified DOM elements are ordered in the DOM at the point of selection (in this case, children of the body tag).

Each item in a selector can then be thought of as consisting of two other objects. The first is the actual DOM element that was identified by the selection, represented by a blue square in the preceding diagram. Inside that square in the image is the DOM element type (div), and the value of its id property.

The second is the datum that D3.js has associated with that DOM element, represented by the green square. In this case, there is no data that is bound at this point by D3.js, so the data for each is null (or empty in the diagram). This is because these DOM elements were created in HTML and not with D3.js, and hence there is no associated datum.

Let's change that and bind some data to these div tags. We do this by chaining a call to .data() immediately following the selection functions. This function is passed a collection of values or objects, and it informs D3.js that you want to associate each datum with a specific visual representation created by the function calls that follow.

To demonstrate this, let's modify the code to the following, binding the array of integers to the div tags:

```
var selector = d3.select('body')
                .selectAll('div')
                .data([10, 20, 30, 40]);
```

bl.ock (2.9): http://goo.gl/h101wX. The output is omitted from the book as it is not visually different from the previous example.

The result of chaining the call to .data() tells D3.js that for each item identified in the selector, the datum at the same index in the data should be assigned. In this example, this does not change the visual. It simply assigns a datum to each div element.

To check this, let's examine the result using the developer tools. If you right-click on **A** in the browser, and select inspect item, the tools will open. Next, open the properties panel, as shown in the following screenshot:

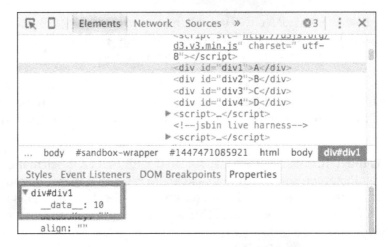

The highlighted red rectangle in the preceding screenshot shows that the div tag now has a __data__ property, and its value is 10. This is how D3.js binds data to the visuals, by creating this property on the DOM element and assigning the datum. If you examine the three other div tags, you will see that they all have this property and the associated value.

Using the visual for our selector, we get the following values:

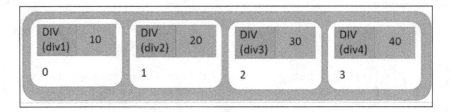

Now you might ask what happens if the count of items in the call to .data() does not equal the amount of items in the selector? Let's take a look at those scenarios, starting with the case of fewer data items than the selected DOM elements:

```
var selector = d3.select('body')
                  .selectAll('div')
                  .data([10, 20, 30]);
```

bl.ock (2.10): http://goo.gl/89NReN. The output has been omitted again, since the visual did not change.

If you open the Developer tools after running this example, and examine the properties for each of our div tags, you will notice that the first three have a __data__ property with the values assigned. The fourth tag does not have the property added. This is because D3.js iterates through the items in the data, assigning them one by one, and any extra DOM elements in the selector are ignored.

Conceptually, the selector then looks like following:

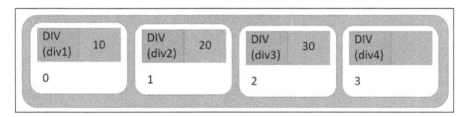

Now let's change the code to have more data items than the DOM elements:

```
var selector = d3.select('body')
                  .selectAll('div')
                  .data([10, 20, 30, 40, 50]);
```

bl.ock (2.11): http://goo.gl/CvuxNJ. The output has been omitted again since the visual did not change.

Examining the resulting DOM in the Developer tools, you can see that there are still only four `div` elements, with `10` through `40` assigned respectively. There is no new visual created for the extra data item.

```
▼ <body>
    <script src="http://d3js.org/d3.v3.min.js" charset=" utf-8"></script>
    <div id="div1">A</div>
    <div id="div2">B</div>
    <div id="div3">C</div>
    <div id="div4">D</div>
```

Why is a visual not created in this case? It is because the call to `.data()` assigns data only to the existing visual elements in the selector. Since `.data()` iterates the items passed to it, it stops at the last item, and the extra DOM elements are ignored.

 We will examine how we add visuals for these stray data items in the next section.

There is one more case that I think is worth examining. The examples so far for `.data()` have had pre-existing `div` tags in the document. Let's now try binding some data items when there are no existing `div` tags. The body of code for this is as follows:

```
var selector = d3.select('body')
                .selectAll('div')
                .data([10, 20, 30]);
```

 bl.ock (2.12): `http://goo.gl/5gsEGe`. The output has been omitted as there are no visuals.

This does not create any DOM elements, since we do not chain any functions to create them after `.data()`. However, the variable selector is a valid selector with three items. In our visual, it would look like the following diagram, where the blue squares are empty:

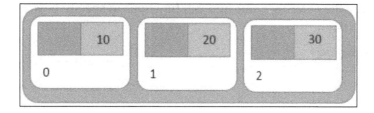

If you take a look at the output created on the console, you will see that this selector indeed has an array of three items:

```
[[undefined, undefined, undefined]]
```

The output does not necessarily show the data, but it does demonstrate that the selector consists of three items. Our conceptual model shows more, but it is only a conceptual model after all, and intended for understanding and not for representing the underlying data structures.

Now let's see how we instruct D3.js to create some visuals for the data items to fill in those blue squares, and put something on the screen.

Specifying the entering elements with .enter()

To create visuals with D3.js, we need to call the .enter() method of the selector after the call to .data(). Then we chain the other method calls to append one or more DOM elements, and normally, also call various functions for setting the properties of those DOM elements.

To exemplify the use of .enter(), let's take a look at the last example from the previous section, where we started without any div tags in the body and used D3.js to bind three integers:

```
var selector = d3.select('body')
    .selectAll('div')
    .data([10, 20, 30]);
```

Now using the selector variable, we call the .enter() function and assign it to a variable named entering:

```
var entering = selector.enter();
```

The value of entering will represent the new items in the selector that need to be created. selector did not have any div tags selected, and since we bound to three items, this variable represents the three new items in the selector that need to be created.

We can then use the entering value and call functions to specify how to render the visuals for each item:

```
entering.append('div')
    .text(function(d) { return d; });
```

 bl.ock (2.13): http://goo.gl/HFdspR.

After execution, the value of `selector` contains three items, with both values assigned and the DOM elements created:

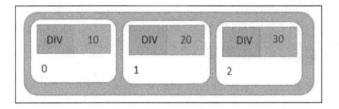

The resulting output on the page will be as follows:

```
10
20
30
```

Examining the resulting DOM, we see that three `div` tags have been created:

```
▼ <body>
    <script src="http://d3js.org/
    d3.v3.min.js" charset=" utf-8"></script>
  ▶ <script>...</script>
    <div>10</div>
    <div>20</div>
    <div>30</div>
```

I will leave it as an exercise for you to examine the properties of these elements for verifying the creation of the __data__ property and assignment of the values.

Adding new items using .enter()

Now that we have created DOM elements from data without any existing visuals, let's change the code to update the data by adding a new datum upon the press of a button.

In D3.js, data which need new visuals created are said to be in a state referred to as *entering*. After calling `.data()`, we can call the `.enter()` method on that same resulting selector. This method identifies the items in the selector that are entering, and hence require visuals to be created. We then simply chain methods on the result of `.enter()` to tell D3.js how each data item should be visualized.

Let's change our code a little bit to demonstrate this in action.

 bl.ock (2.14): `http://goo.gl/TuVYQu`

This code makes a few modifications to the previous example. First we add a button that can be pressed. This button will call a function named `render()` and pass an array of four values to it, the first three of which are identical in value. There also exists a new datum at the end:

```
<button onclick='render([10, 20, 30, 40])'>Take action!</button>
```

The render function itself does the selection and creation of the new visual elements, but it uses the values passed to the function instead of a hard-coded array of values.

```
function render(dataToRender) {
  var selector = d3.select('body')
                   .selectAll('div')
                   .data(dataToRender);

  var entering = selector.enter();
  entering.append('div')
          .text(function(d) { return d; });
}
```

When the page is first loaded, we call render, telling it to create elements in a different array.

```
render([10, 20, 30]);
```

The initial page that is loaded will contain the following content:

> Take action!
> 10
> 20
> 30

When we press the button we call render again, but pass it four values. This results in the content on the page changing as follows:

> Take action!
> 10
> 20
> 30
> 40

This may appear as if the previously existing `div` tags were replaced with four new ones, but what happens is actually more subtle. The second time that `render()` is called, the call to `.selectAll('div')` creates a selector that has three items, each of which has DOM elements and their bound data:

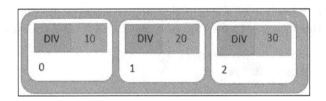

Then, `.data([10, 20, 30, 40])` is executed. D3.js iterates this array, and it compares the value of each datum to the item in the selector at the same index. In this case, the items at positions 0, 1, and 2 have the values `10`, `20`, and `30`, which are each equal to the values at the same position in the data. Therefore, D3.js does not do anything to these items. But the fourth value, `40`, does not have an associated item in the selector.

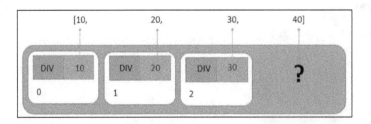

Therefore, D3.js will create a new item in the selector for the datum 40, and then apply the functions for creating the visuals, resulting in the following:

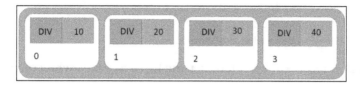

D3.js has left the first three items (and their DOM elements) untouched, and added new DOM elements for just the 40 datum.

 One thing to point out in this example is that I did not set the ID property, and hence the conceptual selector does not show the property.

Updating values

Now let's look at an example where we change the value of several of the items in our data. In this case, we do not want to remove and insert a new visual in the DOM, but to simply update the properties in the DOM to represent a change in the underlying values.

 An example of an update like this could be the price of a stock that needs to be updated.

To demonstrate this, let's make a quick change to the previous example, where when we click the button, we will now execute the following:

```
<button onclick='render([20, 30, 50])'>Take action!</button>
```

 bl.ock (2.15): http://goo.gl/nyUrRL On pressing the button, we get the following result:

Take action!
10
20
30

Nothing has changed on the page! Shouldn't the page be displaying 20, 30, and 50?

This gets into some of the subtleties of D3.js data binding. Let's step through this to explain this result:

```
var selector = d3.select('body')
    .selectAll('div')
    .data(dataToRender);
```

The call to `.selectAll('div')` identifies the three `div` tags when the page was loaded:

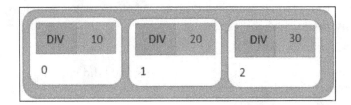

Following that, the call to `.data()` binds new values to each item in the selector:

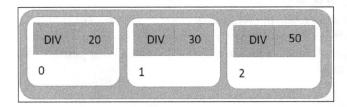

D3.js has changed the bound values, but all the items were reused, and hence, are not tagged as entering. Therefore, the following statement results in an empty set of entering items.

```
var entering = selector.enter();
```

As a result, the chained methods are not executed, and the DOM elements are not updated.

How do we fix this? It's actually quite simple: we need to handle both, the case of entering elements and the case of the already existing ones. To do this, change the render function to the following:

```
function render(dataToRender) {
    var selector = d3.select('body')
        .selectAll('div')
        .data(dataToRender);

    var entering = selector.enter();
```

```
entering.append('div')
    .text(function(d) { return d; });

selector.text(function(d) { return d; });
}
```

The only difference is that we have added the following line:

```
selector.text(function(d) { return d; });
```

When we chain methods to the original selector, the chained functions will be applied to all the items in the selector that are neither entering nor exiting (we cover exiting in the next section). And the result is what we expected:

```
Take action!
20
30
50
```

Removing items with .exit()

Now let's discuss how visuals change when items are removed from the collection of bound data. To handle exit, we simply need to use the `.exit()` function on the result of `.data()`. The return value of `.exit()` is a collection of the selector items which D3.js has determined need removal from the visualization based upon the change in data.

To demonstrate the removal of items, we will make a couple of simple modifications to the previous example. First, let's change the button code to render the following array upon clicking:

```
<button onclick='render([5, 15])'>Take action!</button>
```

When we execute the page with this change, we get the following result:

```
Take action!
5
15
30
```

Conceptually, we would have expected the resulted as a page with just 5 and 15, and not 5, 15, and 30.

The reason for this result is again because of the way that D3.js handles data binding. When we call .data() with the updated data, D3.js attempts to reconcile the following:

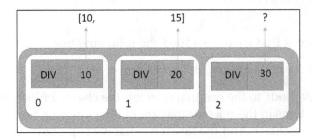

Since all that .data() does is update the bound value in each item of the selector, and since there are fewer values than the selector items, we get the following selector as a result:

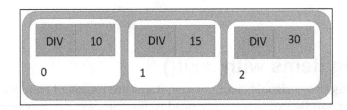

We then call our code to handle the enter and update states. In this case, there are no entering items, whereas items at positions 0 and 1 are scheduled for update. Hence, the first two div tags get new text values, and the third div is left unchanged in the DOM.

All that we have to do to fix this is make a call to .exit(), and use the results of this call to remove those items from the DOM. We can modify render() to the following, which gives us our desired result:

bl.ock (2.16): http://goo.gl/IkIjGY

```
function render(dataToRender) {
    var selector = d3.select('body')
        .selectAll('div')
        .data(dataToRender);

    var entering = selector.enter();
```

```
entering.append('div')
    .text(function(d) { return d; });

selector.text(function(d) { return d; });

var exiting = selector.exit();
exiting.remove();
}
```

The only change is the addition of the last two lines. Now when we press the button, we get the desired result:

A few notes for the wise about the general update pattern

To close this chapter, I'd like to emphasize several points about managing visuals based upon data using D3.js. I believe these will definitely help you avoid problems in learning D3.js. Having come from other development platforms where data binding works in a different manner, I definitely struggled with these issues, and I want to pass along the insights that have I have learned to save you a lot of stress. It's kind of a long list, but I believe it to be very valuable.

- A visualization is almost always based upon data, and is not just coded explicitly.

- Normally, a D3.js application, on page load, will perform a `.selectAll()` on the document for the DOM elements that would represent data. Often, the result of this selection does not have any elements, as the page was just loaded.

- A call is then made to `.data()` to bind data to the selector that results from the selection.

- `.data()` iterates across the datum that are passed to it, and ensures that there are items in the selector to correlate the datum to the visuals. The value of the datum is copied into this item. DOM elements are not created by the call to `.data()`.

- Data in many apps changes dynamically over time without reloading the page, either by user interaction or through code that updates the data based upon other events. You would want to update the visualization when this happens. Therefore, you will need to call .data() multiple times.

- If the number of items in the data is more than the number of items in the selector it is applied to, then more selector items will be created at the end of the selector. These will be marked as in a state referred to as entering. These will be accessible using the .enter() function on the selector. You then chain the function calls to create DOM elements for each new item in the selector.

- If the number of items in the data is less than the number of items in the selector, then selector items will be removed from the end of the selector. These will be marked as exiting. These selector items will be available through a call to the .exit() function. These DOM elements will not be removed from the DOM automatically, and you will need to make a call to .remove() to make this so.

- To optimize this process, D3.js really only concerns itself with ensuring the number of items in the selector matches the number of datum that you specify with .data().

- The data associated with a selector item is by value and not reference. Hence, .data() copies data into the __data__ property on the DOM element. On subsequent calls to .data(), there is no comparison performed between the datum and the value of the __data__ property.

- To update data, you write code to chain methods for generating DOM on the result of a selection, in addition to code that chains on the .enter() and .exit() functions.

- If a new datum has the same value as is already associated to a selector item, D3.js does not care. Even though the values have not changed, you will be rendering it again, but reusing the DOM elements. You will need to provide your own facilities to manage not setting the properties again if the data is the same, so as to optimize the browser re-rendering the elements.

- If you have 1,000,000 data items, and then change just one and call .data() again, D3.js will inherently force you to loop through all the 1,000,000 items. There will likely be visual updates to just one set of visuals, but your application will make the effort to iterate through everything every time. However, if you have 1,000,000 data items, you probably should be looking at another means of summarizing your data before visualizing it.

- D3.js optimizes around the reuse of visual elements. The assumption is that a visualization will only be periodically making updates to the exiting items, and that addition or removal of items will be relatively infrequent. Hence, the general update pattern would consist of exit, update, and exit, and not comparing data.

- Normally, the rule of thumb is that one or two thousand data items and the associated visuals are handled pretty effectively by D3.js.

Well, that's quite a long list. But as we progress through this book, all the examples will follow these guidelines. By the end, these will be second nature.

Summary

In this chapter, we covered many examples to demonstrate how you can create data-driven visualizations using D3.js. We started with examples of the D3.js concept of selectors, using them to select elements from within the DOM, and discussed how selectors are used to map data items to the visuals that D3.js creates. We then examined several scenarios of binding new data, updating data, and removing data from a D3.js visualization.

Throughout this chapter, the visuals that we created with D3.js were pure HTML objects, primarily `div` tags. Although we changed the size of these `div` tags, the background color, and included text within them, the examples are a very basic form of graphical representation.

In the next chapter, we will start to get significantly more graphical by changing the focus of the examples towards working with SVG, creating real graphics (not just HTML `div` tags), and setting a framework for the rich visualizations that we will create later in the book.

3

Creating Visuals with SVG

In this chapter, we will learn about **Scalable Vector Graphics**, commonly referred to as **SVG**. SVG is a web standard for creating vector-based graphics within the browser. We will begin the chapter with several basic examples of directly coding SVG within the browser, and in the end, examine how to use D3 to create SVG elements based on data.

In this chapter, we will cover the following topics:

- A brief introduction to SVG, coordinates, and attributes
- A simple example of SVG that draws circles
- Working with fundamental shapes: ellipses, rectangles, lines, and paths
- The relationship of CSS with SVG and D3.js
- Using strokes, line caps, and dashes
- Fundamental transformations: rotate, translate, and scale
- Grouping SVG elements and uniformly applying transforms
- Transparency and layering of SVG elements

Introducing SVG

Up to this point, we have used D3 to create new DIV elements in the DOM. While many great visualizations can be created using D3 and DIVs, the true expressive power of D3 lies in using it to create and manipulate SVG elements.

SVG is an XML markup language that has been designed to express very rich 2D visualizations. SVG can take advantage of the computer's graphics processor to accelerate rendering, and is also optimized for user interaction and animation.

Instead of directly manipulating the pixels on the screen, SVG uses vectors for building a model of the presentation, and then transforms this representation into pixels on your behalf. This makes coding of visualizations much simpler as compared to other web technologies such as HTML5 Canvas.

Since the image is stored as a vector-based representation, the visualization of the model can be scalable. This is because all the visual elements can be easily scaled (both larger and smaller) without resulting in visual artifacts as a result of the scaling.

SVG has a convenience in that its language can be used directly within HTML on browsers that support SVG. D3 provides direct support and manipulation of SVG with D3, which feels exactly like manipulating the DOM with D3.

The SVG coordinate system

The coordinate system of SVG has an origin in the upper-left corner of the SVG element, which is **(0,0)**; the value of x increases towards the right, while those of y increase towards the bottom. This is common in computer graphics systems, but can occasionally be confusing for those used to mathematical graphs where the origin is in the lower-left or dead center.

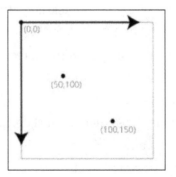

SVG attributes

SVG, while being able to seamlessly integrate with HTML, is not HTML. Specifically, properties and styles may operate differently. An example of this is that where most HTML elements have width and height elements, but not all SVG elements use these properties.

A second important point about SVG is that the position of an element is set through attributes. Due to this, it is not possible to set the position of the SVG elements using a style. Additionally, to change the position of an SVG element, such as within an animation, it is necessary to have code which sets the properties for positioning the element.

Drawing circles with SVG

We work with SVG within HTML by using an SVG tag, and placing the SVG elements within that tag. A very simple example is the following, which creates three circles:

```
<svg width="720" height="120">
    <circle cx="40" cy="20" r="10"></circle>
    <circle cx="80" cy="40" r="15"></circle>
    <circle cx="120" cy="60" r="20"></circle>
</svg>
```

This results in the following image within the browser:

[ bl.ock (3.1): `http://goo.gl/UMCLt1`]

The SVG element itself is not visible on the page, and only provides a holder for the child tags. In this book, we will always explicitly set the width and heights of the SVG tag. In this example, it is set to be `720` pixels wide by `120` pixels tall.

The positioning of a circle within an SVG element is performed by specifying the center x and y values of the circle. This location is relative to the upper-left corner of the SVG element, with positive x values moving to the right from the origin, and positive y values moving downwards. The size of the circle is specified by the `r` attribute, which indicates the radius of the circle.

The example did not specify a color for these circles, so the default color of the circles is black. Most SVG elements specify the color by using the CSS style attribute, and then by setting the `fill` attribute of the style.

For example, the following code gives different colors (red, green and blue) to the three circles:

```
<svg width="720" height="120">
  <circle cx="40" cy="20" r="10" style="fill:red"></circle>
  <circle cx="80" cy="40" r="15" style="fill:green"></circle>
  <circle cx="120" cy="60" r="20" style="fill:blue"></circle>
</svg>
```

This results in the following output:

bl.ock (3.2): `http://goo.gl/2k1ZIm`

D3 selections work identically with SVG elements as they do with the DOM elements. As a quick example, the following selects all the circles within the selected `svg` tag, and sets their colors to a uniform `teal` color.

```
<svg width="720" height="120">
  <circle cx="40" cy="20" r="10" style="fill:red"></circle>
  <circle cx="80" cy="40" r="15" style="fill:green"></circle>
  <circle cx="120" cy="60" r="20" style="fill:blue"></circle>
</svg>
<script>
  d3.selectAll('circle').style('fill', 'teal');
</script>
```

This results in the following output within the browser:

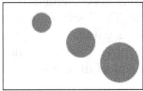

bl.ock (3.3): `http://goo.gl/bszmEf`

The basic shapes provided by SVG

Having some preliminaries out of the way, let's now examine the various SVG shapes that we will commonly use through the book. We have already seen how to create a circle; now let's look at some other shapes.

Ellipse

A circle is a special case of an ellipse that has an identical x and y radii. Ellipses can and often have different size radii. An ellipse is specified in SVG using the `<ellipse>` tag. We still use `cx` and `cy` attributes to position the ellipse, but instead of using `r` for radius, we use two attributes `rx` and `ry` to specify the radius in the x and y directions:

```
<ellipse cx="50" cy="30" rx="40" ry="20" />
```

 bl.ock (3.4): http://goo.gl/05QCnG

Rectangle

Rectangles are specified using the `<rect>` tag. The upper-left corner is specified using the `x` and `y` attributes. The `width` and `height` attributes specify those respective sizes for the rectangle:

```
<rect x="10" y="10" width="150" height="100"></rect>
```

 bl.ock (3.5): http://goo.gl/b3w1Rq

Lines

It is possible to draw lines with SVG using the `<line>` tag. A line requires at least four attributes to be specified, and normally uses five. The first two, x1 and y1, specify the starting position of the line. Two more attributes, x2 and y2, specify the end point for the line. The last property, albeit not required, is stroke, which specifies the color to be used to draw the line. Usually, we must specify the stroke to actually see the line. Here we set it to black.

```
<line x1="10" y1="10" x2="100" y2="100" stroke="black" />
```

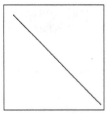

bl.ock (3.6): `http://goo.gl/4qZejC`

Paths

Paths are one of the most powerful drawing constructs in SVG. They provide a symbolic notion that can be used to create many geometries. A path can be shapes such as circles and rectangles. Paths also provide the user the ability to create curves using control points.

The drawing of the path is controlled by specifying one attribute, d, which is passed a string that specifies drawing commands that will be executed.

The basic concept of a path is that you can draw a series of either straight or curved lines, and then have the option of filling the space inside if the shape is closed. For example, the following command creates a triangle filled with black color:

```
<path d="M 10 10 L 310 20 L 160 110 Z"/>
```

bl.ock (3.7): http://goo.gl/kCTbv7

A path usually starts with an M command, which starts drawing at that specific location, in this case (10, 10). The next command, L 310 10, draws a from the previous point to (310, 10). The next command, L 160 10, then draws a line from (310, 10) to (160, 10). The final command is Z, which tells SVG that the shape is closed. Essentially, this informs SVG that there is an implicit line to the first position in the string of commands, in this case (10, 10).

Note that we did not specify a fill or stroke color. These default to black in a path.

The mini-language for paths is quite robust, and therefore, also complex. The following table lists several other common path commands:

Command	Purpose
M	Move-to
L	Line-to
H	Horizontal line-to
V	Veritcal line-to
C	Curve-to
Q	Quadractic Bezier curve-to
T	Smooth quadratic Bezier curve-to
A	Elliptical arc
Z	Close path

D3 provides a number of tools to facilitate the use of paths that make them much simpler to use compared to manually specifying them with string literals. We will examine a few of those later in the chapter.

Text

The <text> SVG tag allows us to place text within the SVG element. The placing of text within an SVG is different than the way it is done in HTML. The SVG text items are drawn with vector graphics instead of being rasterized. Hence, text rendered in SVG is more flexible than the rasterized text rendered with HTML. Curves in letters rendered with SVG remain smooth instead of becoming pixelated when zoom levels are applied to the entire graphic.

Text is positioned using the x and y attributes, which specify the **baseline** of the text be located at y and the text to be left-justified to x, the bottom baseline of the text (the portion at the bottom of the main part of the letters, excluding the descenders) left of the text being the anchor of the positioning.

This is demonstrated by the following, which also sets the font family, size and fill color. The actual text to be displayed is set with the inner text content of the tag:

```
<text x="10" y="20"
      fill="Red" font-family="arial" font-size="16">
  Content of the SVG text
</text>
```

Which renders the following in the upper-left side of the SVG element:

Content of the SVG text

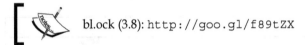 bl.ock (3.8): `http://goo.gl/f89tZX`

Applying CSS styles to SVG elements

SVG elements can be styled identically to the way HTML elements are styled. The same CSS with ID and class attributes can be used to direct styles to the SVG elements, or you can just use the style attribute directly and specify CSS as its content. However, many of the actual styles in HTML differ in SVG. For example, SVG uses `fill` for a rectangle, whereas HTML would use background for a `div` tag that represents a rectangle.

In this book, we will generally try to avoid using CSS, and explicitly code the style attributes using the functions provided by D3.js. But many examples on the web do use CSS combined with SVG, so it is worth a quick mention.

The following example demonstrates styling SVG with CSS. The example uses two styles to set the fills of several rectangles. The first style will make all the rectangles red by default. The second one defines a style that makes all the rectangles with ID `willBeGreen` filled with green color. The example then creates three rectangles: the first two using the CSS styles, and the third using CSS within the style `attributeset` as fill to `blue`.

bl.ock (3.9): `http://goo.gl/KAnc6j`

The styles defined in the sample are the following:

```
<style>
    svg rect { fill: red; }
    svg rect#willBeGreen { fill: green; }
</style>
```

And the rectangles are created as follows:

```
<rect x="10" y="10" width="50" height="50" />
<rect x="70" y="10" width="50" height="50" id="willBeGreen" />
<rect x="130" y="10" width="50" height="50" style="fill:blue" />
```

The resulting output will be as shown in the following image:

Strokes, caps, and dashes

SVG shapes have an attribute known as `stroke`. The attribute `stroke` specifies the color of a line that outlines an SVG shape. We saw the use of stroke with a line, but it can be used with most of the SVG elements.

Whenever we specify `stroke`, we usually also specify a stroke width using the `stroke-width` attribute. This informs SVG about the thickness (in pixels) of the outline that will be rendered.

To demonstrate `stroke` and `stroke-width` attributes, the following example recreates the path from the path example, and sets a stroke to be `10` pixels thick, using `red` as its color. Additionally, we set the `fill` of the path to `blue`. We set all the attributes using the `style` property of `stroke`:

```
<path d="M 10 10 L 210 10 L 110 120 z"
      style="fill:blue;stroke:red;stroke-width:5" />
```

The preceding example results in the following rendering:

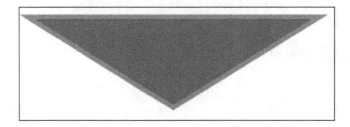

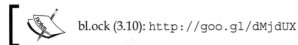

bl.ock (3.10): `http://goo.gl/dMjdUX`

As we saw earlier, we can set stroke on a line. It can also have its `stroke-width` set. Let's examine this by changing our line example to set the thickness of the line to `20` and the color to `green`:

```
<line x1="10" y1="10" x2="110" y2="110"
        stroke="green" stroke-width="20" />
```

bl.ock (3.11): `http://goo.gl/p880dC`

Notice how this line actually looks like a rectangle. This is because lines have an attribute named `stroke-linecap` which describes the shape of the end of the line, known as the line cap.

The default for this value is butt, which gives us the 90 degree sharp corners. The other values that can be used are square or round. The following example demonstrates the same line with all these different stroke-linecap values:

```
<line x1="10" y1="20" x2="110" y2="100"
      stroke="red" stroke-width="20" stroke-linecap="butt" />
<line x1="60" y1="20" x2="160" y2="100"
      stroke="green" stroke-width="20" stroke-linecap="square" />
<line x1="110" y1="20" x2="210" y2="100"
      stroke="blue" stroke-width="20" stroke-linecap="round" />
<path d="M 10 20 L 110 100 M 60 20 L 160 100 M 110 20 L 210 100"
      stroke="white" />
```

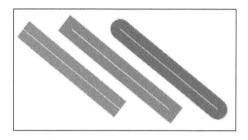

bl.ock (3.12): http://goo.gl/Xcaz41

Note that for each of the three lines, we drew a line with a stroke-width of 20, and then within each line, we drew a white line using a single path with three move and line commands. The white line helps in distinguishing the effect of the end caps on the lines.

First examine the red line. The ends are flush with the end of the white line. Contrast it with the green line. In this line, the line-cap, still square, extends past the white line by the width of the stroke. The blue line, with a round line-cap, is drawn using a half circle of radius of one half of the stroke-width.

By default, the SVG lines are solid, but they can also be created with dashes, specified by using the `stroke-dasharray` attribute. This attribute is given a list of integer values which specify a repeating pattern of line segment widths, the first starting with the `stroke` color and alternating with empty space:

```
<line x1="10" y1="20" x2="110" y2="120"
        stroke="red" stroke-width="5"
        stroke-dasharray="5,5" />
<line x1="60" y1="20" x2="160" y2="120"
        stroke="green" stroke-width="5"
        stroke-dasharray="10,10" />
<line x1="110" y1="20" x2="210" y2="120"
        stroke="blue" stroke-width="5"
        stroke-dasharray="20,10,5,5,5" />
```

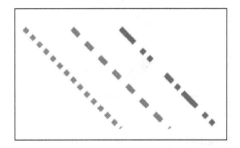

bl.ock (3.13): `http://goo.gl/VyBBwy`

Applying SVG transforms

The **S** in SVG stands for **Scalable**, while **V** stands for **Vector**. These are the two important parts of the name. This allows us to be able to apply a variety of transforms prior to the rendering of SVG shapes.

Each SVG shape is represented by one or more vectors, where a vector in SVG is a tuple (x, y) distance from an origin in the coordinate system. As an example, a rectangle will be represented by four 2D vectors, one for each corner of the rectangle.

When creating graphical visualizations, this modeling of data with vectors has several benefits. One of those is that we can define a shape around a coordinate system for just that shape. Modeling this way allows us to make copies of the shape, but position them in different places in a larger image, rotate them, scale them, and perform many other operations beyond the scope of this text.

Secondly, these transformations are applied on the model before being rendered into pixels on the screen. Because of this, SVG can ensure that irrespective of the level of scale applied to the image, it does not get pixelated.

Another important concept in transformations is that they can be applied in a chain and in any sequence. This is an extremely powerful concept in linear algebra for creating composite models of visuals.

There are many ramifications of the transformations and their sequencing that can take effect on the result of the rendering in SVG. Unfortunately, an explanation of these is beyond the scope of the book, but when they have an effect on examples, we will examine them in light of that particular example.

In this section, and in other examples in this book, we will use three general types of transformations provided by SVG: `translate`, `rotate`, and `scale`. Transformations can be applied to an SVG element by using the `transform` attribute.

To demonstrate transforms, we will look at several examples that apply each transform to a rectangle to see how they affect the resulting rendering of the rectangle.

Rotate

The first transformation that we will examine is rotation. We can rotate an SVG object by a specified number of degrees using `.rotate(x)`, where x specifies the number of degrees to rotate the element.

To demonstrate this, the following example rotates our rectangle by 45 degrees. A simple axis with two lines is rendered to give a frame of reference for the translation. This will be included in this code snippet, but excluded in the rest for brevity:

```
<line x1="0" y1="150" x2="0" y2="0" stroke="black" />
<line x1="0" y1="0" x2="150" y2="0" stroke="black" />
<rect x="0" y="0 " width="100" height="100" fill="red"
      transform="rotate(45)" />
```

The preceding snippet gives us the folllowing result:

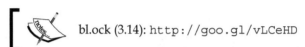

bl.ock (3.14): `http://goo.gl/vLCeHD`

This is not quite the effect that we may have wanted. This is because the rotation of a rectangle is performed around its upper-left corner. To make this appear to have rotated around its center, we need to use an alternate form of `rotate()` which takes three parameters: the angle to rotate followed by an offset from the upper-left corner of the rectangle to a point that represents the center of the rectangle:

```
<rect x="0" y="0" width="100" height="100" fill="red"
      transform="rotate(45,50,50)" />
```

bl.ock (3.15): `http://goo.gl/ujF3iY`

The rectangle has now been rotated about its center, but there is an issue of several of the corners being clipped outside the bounds of the containing SVG element. We will fix this when we look at translations in the next section.

Translate

An SVG element can be repositioned within its containing element by using a **transformation**. A transform is performed using the `translate()` function. `translate()` takes two values: the distance in x and y and the distance to reposition the element within its parent.

The following example will draw our rectangle, and translate it 30 pixels to the right and 30 pixels down:

```
<rect x="0" y="0 " width="100" height="100" fill="red"
        transform="translate(30,30)" />
```

bl.ock (3.16): `http://goo.gl/jANiXU`

Now let's look back at the last rotation example, where two of the corners of the rectangle were clipped. We can fix this to see those corners by specifying a translation on the rectangle to move it right and down 30 pixels prior to the rotation:

```
<rect x="0" y="0" width="100" height="100" fill="red"
        transform="translate(30,30) rotate(45,50,50)" />
```

bl.ock (3.17): `http://goo.gl/W6MeSc`

This also demonstrates applying multiple transformations within a single string supplied to transform. You can sequentially apply many transforms in this manner to handle complex modeling scenarios.

 A common question about translate transform is why not just change the *x* and *y* attributes to position the elements instead of using the transform?

The answer to this can be very complicated and has many reasons. The first is that not all SVG elements are positioned with *x* and *y* attributes, for example, a circle, which is positioned using its *cx* and *cy* attributes. Hence, there is no consistent set of attributes for positioning. Using a translate transform therefore allows us to have a uniform means of positioning the SVG elements no matter what type they are.

Another reason is that when applying multiple transforms, it is not easy (or possible) to access the *x* and *y* attributes. Moreover, through various transforms, the actual location of an SVG element may not match directly with the pixels or points specified in another coordinate system which using *x* and *y* attributes be included.

Scale

Scaling an object changes its apparent visual size by a given percentage along both the *x* and *y* axes. Scaling is performed using the `scale()` function. It can be uniformly applied to each axis, or you can also specify a different scale value for each.

The following example demonstrates scaling. We will draw two rectangles, one atop the other. The rectangle at the bottom will be blue, and the one on top, red. The red will then be scaled to 50 percent of its size:

```
<rect x="0" y="0" width="100" height="100" fill="blue"/>
<rect x="0" y="0" width="100" height="100" fill="red"
      transform="scale(0.5)" />
```

bl.ock (3.18): `http://goo.gl/fCAhg7`

Groups

SVG elements can be grouped together using the `<g>` tag. Any transformations applied to the group will be applied to each of the elements in the group. This is convenient for applying an overall transform to a particular group of items only.

The following example demonstrates both the translation of a group of items (the blue rectangle with text) and the way the transform on the group affects both the items. Note that the green rectangle is not affected because it is not part of the transform:

```
<g transform="translate(100,30) rotate(45 50 50)">
  <rect x="0" y="0" width="100" height="100" style="fill:blue" />
  <text x="15" y="58" fill="White" font-family="arial"
        font-size="16">
        In the box
    </text>
</g>
```

bl.ock (3.19): `http://goo.gl/FY6q4D`

Also notice that the placement of the text on top of the rectangle is relative to the top-left corner of the group, not the SVG element. This is important for ensuring that the text rotates properly relative to the blue rectangle.

Transparency

SVG supports drawing of transparent elements. This can be done by either setting the `opacity` attribute or by using the `rgba (red-green-blue-alpha)` value when specifying a color.

The following example renders three circles of different colors, all of which are 50 percent transparent. The first two use the opacity attribute, and the third uses a transparent color specification for the fill.

```
<circle cx="150" cy="150" r="100"
        style="fill:red" opacity="0.5" />
<circle cx="250" cy="150" r="100"
        style="fill:green" opacity="0.5" />
<circle cx="200" cy="250" r="100"
        style="fill:rgba(0, 0, 255, 0.5)" />
```

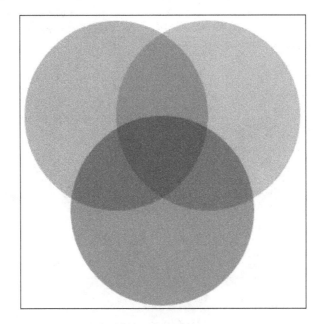

bl.ock (3.20): `http://goo.gl/xRzArg`

Layers

You may have noticed that the SVG elements overlay each other in a particular order, with certain elements appearing to be closer and obscuring those that are behind. Let's examine this using an example that overlays three circles on top of each other:

```
<circle cx="150" cy="150" r="100" style="fill:red" />
<circle cx="250" cy="150" r="100" style="fill:green" />
<circle cx="200" cy="250" r="100" style="fill:blue" />
```

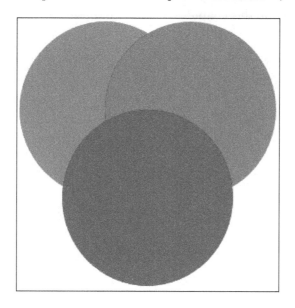

 bl.ock (3.21): http://goo.gl/hO4xmc

The blue circle is drawn in front of the green circle, which is drawn in front of the red circle. This order is defined by the sequence that is specified in the SVG markup, with each successive element being rendered atop the previous elements.

> If you have used other graphics packages or UI tools, you would know that they often provide a concept known as a Z-order, with Z being a pseudo-dimension where the drawing order of the elements is from the lowest to the highest Z-order. SVG does not offer this ability, but we will see in later chapters that we can address this by sorting the selections before laying them out.

Summary

In this chapter, you learned how to use SVG to create various shapes, how to lay out the SVG elements using the SVG coordinates, and how layers affect the rendering. You also learned to perform transformation on SVG elements, which will be used frequently in examples throughout this book and form an essential part of creating visuals using D3.

In the next chapter, we move back to a focus on D3.js, and in particular we will take what we have learned in this chapter with SVG and use D3 to create a data-driven bar graph using D3.js selections and SVG elements.

4
Creating a Bar Graph

Now that we have examined binding data and generating SVG visuals with D3, we will turn our attention to creating a bar graph using SVG in this chapter. The examples in this chapter will utilize an array static of integers, and use that data to calculate the height of bars, their positions, add labels to the bars, and add margins and axes to the graph to assist the user in understanding the relationships in the data.

In this chapter, we will cover the following topics:

- Creating a series of bars that are bound to data
- Calculating the position and height of the bars
- Using a group to uniformly position multiple elements representing a bar
- Adding margins to the graph
- Creating and manipulating the style and labels in an axis
- Adding an axis to the graph

The basic bar graph

We have explored everything that we need to draw a series of bars based upon data in the first three chapters. The first example in this chapter will leverage using SVG rectangles for drawing the bars. What we need to do now is calculate the size and position of the bars based upon the data.

The code for our bar graph is available at the following location. Open this link in your browser, and we will walk through how the code creates the visual that follows.

bl.ock (4.1): `http://goo.gl/TQo2sX`

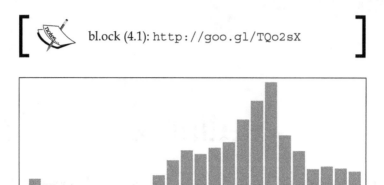

The code starts with a declaration of the data that is to be represented as a graph. This example uses a hard-coded array of integers. We will look at more complex data types later in the book; for now, we simply start with this to get used to the process of binding and that of creating the bars:

```
var data = [55, 44, 30, 23, 17, 14, 16, 25, 41, 61, 85,
            101, 95, 105, 114, 150, 180, 210, 125, 100, 71,
            75, 72, 67];
```

Now we define two variables that define the width of each bar and the amount of spacing between each bar:

```
var barWidth = 15, barPadding = 3;
```

We need to scale the height of each bar relative to the maximum value in the data. This is determined by using the d3.max() function.

```
var maxValue = d3.max(data);
```

Now we create the main SVG element by placing it inside the body of the document, and assign a width and height that we know will hold our visual. Finally, and as a matter of practice that will be used throughout this book, we will append a top-level group element in the SVG tag. We will then place our bars within this group instead of placing them directly in the SVG element:

```
var graphGroup = d3.select('body')
    .append('svg')
    .attr({ width: 1000, height: 250 })
    .append('g');
```

I find this practice of using a top-level group useful as it facilitates placing multiple complex visuals in the same SVG, such as in the case of creating a dashboard.

In this example, we are not going to scale the data, and use an assumption that the container is the proper size to hold the graph. We will look at better ways of doing this, as also for calculating the positions of the bars, in *Chapter 5, Using Data and Scales*. We simply strive to keep it simple for the moment.

We need to perform two pieces of math to be able to calculate the x and y location of the bars. We are positioning these bars at pixel locations starting at the bottom and the left of graphGroup. We need two functions to calculate these. The first one calculates the x location of the left side of the bar:

```
function xloc(d, i) { return i * (barWidth + barPadding); }
```

During binding, this will be passed the current datum and its position within the data array. We do not actually need the value for this calculation. We simply calculate a multiple of the sum of the width and padding for the bar based upon the array position.

Since SVG uses an upper-left origin, we need to calculate the distance from the top of the graph as the location from where we start drawing the bar down towards the bottom of the visual:

```
function yloc(d) { return maxValue - d; }
```

When we position each bar, we will use a translate transform that takes advantage of each of these functions. We can facilitate this by declaring a function which, given the current data item and its array position, returns the calculated string for the transform property based upon this data and the functions:

```
function translator(d, i) {
    return "translate(" + xloc(d, i) + "," + yloc(d) + ")";
}
```

All we need to do now is generate the SVG visuals from the data:

```
barGroup.selectAll("rect")
    .data(data)
    .enter()
    .append('rect')
    .attr({
        fill: 'steelblue',
        transform: translator,
        width: barWidth,
        height: function (d) { return d; }
    });
```

Pretty good for just a few lines of code. But all we can tell from the graph is the relative sizes of the data. We need more information than this to get an effective data visualization.

Adding labels to the bars

Now we will add a label holding the value of the datum right at the top of each bar. The code for this example is available at the following link:

The following image demonstrates the resulting visual:

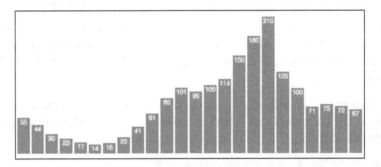

To accomplish this, we will modify our SVG generation such that:

1. Each bar is represented by an SVG group instead of a `rect`.
2. Inside each group that represents a bar, we add an SVG and a text element.
3. The group is then positioned, hence positioning the child elements as well.
4. The size of the `rect` is set as before, causing the containing group to expand to the same size.
5. The text is positioned relative to the upper-left corner of its containing group.

By grouping these elements in this manner, we can reuse the previous code for positioning, and utilize the benefit of the group for locating all the child visuals for a bar. Moreover, we only need to size and position those child elements relative to their own group, making that math very simple. The code for this is identical to the previous example through the declaration of the positioning functions.

The first change is in the creation of the selector that represents the bars:

```
var barGroups = g.selectAll('g')
    .data(data)
    .enter()
    .append('g')
    .attr('transform', translator);
```

Instead of creating a `rect`, the code now creates a group element. The group is initially empty, and it is assigned the transform that moves it into the appropriate position.

Using the selector referred to by `barGroups`, the code now appends a `rect` into each group while also setting the appropriate attributes.

```
barGroups.append('rect')
    .attr({
        fill: 'steelblue',
        width: barWidth,
        height: function(d) { return d; }
    });
```

The next step is to add a `text` element to show the value of the datum. We are going to position this text such that it is right at the top of the bar, and centered in the bar.

To accomplish this, we need a translate transform that represents an offset halfway into the bar and at the top. This is common for each bar, so we can define a variable that is reused for each:

```
var textTranslator = "translate(" + barWidth / 2 + ",0)";
```

Next, the we append a text element into each group, setting its text (the string value of the datum), the appropriate attributes for the text, and finally, the style for the font.

```
barGroups.append('text')
    .text(function(d) { return d; })
    .attr({
        fill: 'white',
        'alignment-baseline': 'before-edge',
        'text-anchor': 'middle',
        transform: textTranslator
    })
    .style('font', '10px sans-serif');
```

That was pretty easy, and it is nice to have the labels on the bars, but our graph could still really use axes. We will look at adding those next.

Margins and axes

Adding axes to the graph will give the reader a much better understanding of the scope of the graph and the relationship between the values in the data. D3.js has very powerful constructs built in for allowing us to create axes.

Axes in D3.js are based upon another concept known as scales. While scales are by themselves very useful (we will cover scales in more detail in *Chapter 5, Using Data and Scales*), for the remainder of this chapter, we will examine using them to create basic axes in our bar chart.

However, before we get to axes, we will first take a short but important diversion into the concept of margins, and that of adding a margin to our bar chart to make room for the axes.

Creating margins in the bar graph

Margins have several practical uses in a graph. They can be used to provide spacing between the graph and other content on the page, giving the reader clean sightlines between their visualization and the other content. However, the real practical use of margins is to provide space on one or more sides of the visualization for providing axes.

The following image demonstrates what we want to accomplish with margins:

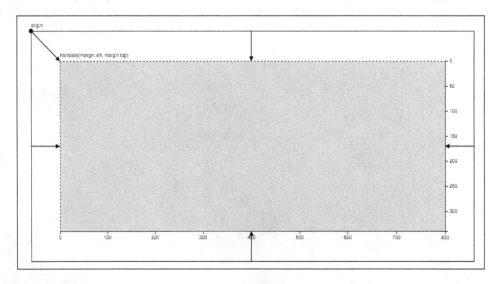

The grey portion is where we will place our existing graph. Then, depending upon the axes that we decide to use (left, top, right, bottom), we need to provide space in our visualization for rendering those axes just outside the graph. Note that a single graph could use any or all of the margins for different axes, so it is a good practice to build code that plans for all of them.

In D3.js applications, this is generally performed using a concept referred to as **margin convention**. We will step through an example of using this concept to add margins to our graph. Additionally, instead of using a static size for our layout, we will compute the height and width of the graph based upon the number of data points in this example.

To get started, load the example from the following information box.

bl.ock (4.3): `http://goo.gl/HTZ2NG`

The resulting visualization for the code is seen in the following graph:

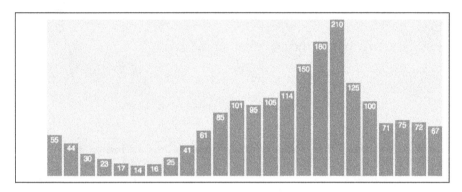

Besides the margins, this example adds a grey background to the area behind the chart. This highlights the area used for the chart, and emphasizes it relative to the margins that are added. It also puts a rectangle around the main SVG element to highlight its boundaries, as it helps us see the extent of the margins added to the graph.

Let's step through this example and examine how it differs from the previous example. We start with calculating the actual width of the area of the bars:

```
var graphWidth = data.length * (barWidth + barPadding)
                 - barPadding;
```

Now we declare a JavaScript object that will represent the size of our margins:

```
var margin = { top: 10, right: 10, bottom: 10, left: 50 };
```

Using these values, we can calculate the total size of the entire visualization:

```
var totalWidth = graphWidth + margin.left + margin.right;
var totalHeight = maxValue + margin.top + margin.bottom;
```

Now we can create the main SVG element, and set it to the exact size that it needs to be:

```
var svg = d3.select('body')
    .append('svg')
    .attr({ width: totalWidth, height: totalHeight });
```

For the visual effect, the following adds a rectangle that shows us the boundaries of the main SVG element:

```
svg.append('rect').attr({
    width: totalWidth,
    height: totalHeight,
    fill: 'white',
    stroke: 'black',
    'stroke-width': 1
});
```

Now we add a group to hold the main part of the graph:

```
var graphGroup = svg
    .append('g')
    .attr('transform', 'translate(' + margin.left + ',' +
                                     margin.top + ")");
```

To emphasize the area of the actual graph, a grey `rect` is added to the group:

```
graphGroup.append('rect').attr({
    fill: 'rgba(0,0,0,0.1)',
    width: totalWidth - (margin.left + margin.right),
    height: totalHeight - (margin.bottom + margin.top)
});
```

The remainder of the code remains the same.

At this point, we have added margins around the graph, and made room on the left side for an axis to be drawn. Before we put that in the visualization, let's first take a look at an example of creating an axis to learn some of the concepts involved.

Creating an axis

To demonstrate the creation of an axis, we will start with creating an axis appropriate for placement at the bottom of the graph, referred to as a **bottom** axis. This is the default type of axis created with D3.js. So we will start with it, and then examine changing the orientation after looking at a few concepts related to axes.

The following is the code for the example that we will walk through, and which results in the generation of the subsequent axis:

bl.ock (4.4): `http://goo.gl/TyDAH6`

)	20	40	60	80	100	120	140	160	180	200

In our example, we create the scale and axis with the following lines of code:

```
var scale = d3.scale
    .linear()
    .domain([0, maxValue])
    .range([0, width]);

var axis = d3.svg.axis().scale(scale);
svg.call(axis);
```

To create an axis, we first need to create a **scale** object using `d3.scale()`. A scale informs the axis about the range of values it will represent (known as the **domain**), and the overall size for which the axis should be rendered in the visual (referred to as the **range**). In this example, we are using a **linear** scale. A linear scale informs the axis that the values will be linearly interpolated from the lower to the higher value, in this case, 0 to 210.

D3.js scales have uses for things other than axes. We will examine these uses in *Chapter 5, Using Data and Scales*.

The axis is then created using the d3.svg.axis() function, and by passing it the scale by chaining a call to .scale().

The axis scale then needs to be associated with a selection, which is performed using the .call() function. This informs D3.js that when it renders the visual that it should call the axis function to render itself.

This feels a little different than the way we have created visual elements so far. This technique is used by D3.js because an axis is a complex set of SVG elements that need to be generated. The use of .call() allows us to separate complex rendering logic into a function call during the rendering pipeline, and the design of D3.js was made to render axes in this manner.

The labels on the axis are automatically generated by D3.js, and are based upon the values of the domain. The visualized size of the axis is specified by the range. In this case, since this is a bottom axis, the labelling starts at the minimum value of 0, and D3.js uses intervals of 20 for the labels. The last label that fits is 200, so D3.js does not actually create a label for the maximum value of 210.

In the output, the label 0 is clipped. This is because the axis is positioned flush to the left of the SVG element. This orientation is such that the line in the axis is flush. Since the text for the first label is center-justified on the tick, its left half gets clipped. This can be fixed easily with a translation, which we will examine when we place the axis next to our graph.

Inspecting the rendered axis using Developer tools, you will see the effort that D3.js has made to generate the axis:

```
▼ <svg width="500" height="500">
  ▼ <g>
    ▶ <g class="tick" transform="translate(0,0)" style="opacity: 1;">…</g>
    ▶ <g class="tick" transform="translate(47.61904761904761,0)" style="opacity: 1;">…</g>
    ▶ <g class="tick" transform="translate(95.23809523809523,0)" style="opacity: 1;">…</g>
    ▶ <g class="tick" transform="translate(142.85714285714286,0)" style="opacity: 1;">…</g>
    ▶ <g class="tick" transform="translate(190.47619047619045,0)" style="opacity: 1;">…</g>
    ▶ <g class="tick" transform="translate(238.09523809523807,0)" style="opacity: 1;">…</g>
    ▶ <g class="tick" transform="translate(285.7142857142857,0)" style="opacity: 1;">…</g>
    ▶ <g class="tick" transform="translate(333.33333333333,0)" style="opacity: 1;">…</g>
    ▶ <g class="tick" transform="translate(380.9523809523809,0)" style="opacity: 1;">…</g>
    ▶ <g class="tick" transform="translate(428.57142857142856,0)" style="opacity: 1;">…</g>
    ▶ <g class="tick" transform="translate(476.19047619047615,0)" style="opacity: 1;">…</g>
      <path class="domain" d="M0,6V0H500V6"></path>
  </g>
</svg>
```

What D3.js has done is generate a group for each tick on the axis and a single path that renders the line of the axis. Each tick group itself consists of a line that represents the tick on the axis and the label on the tick.

Examining the output, you will notice that we do not actually see any ticks along the axis. This makes it difficult to realize the actual point on the axis that is associated with the label. This is due to the default styling that is used. We will make this axis look better in the next section.

The reason we could not see the ticks on our axis is due to the default thickness of the path representing the axis. We can change this by simply modifying the style of the path representing the axis as well as the style of the ticks.

Open the following example in your browser to learn how to accomplish this:

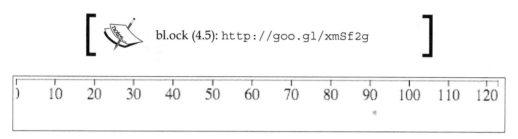

bl.ock (4.5): `http://goo.gl/xmSf2g`

This code makes a few small modifications to be able to change the style as shown in the following section of code:

```
var axisGroup = svg.append('g');
var axis = d3.svg.axis().scale(scale);

var axis = d3.svg.axis().scale(scale);
var axisNodes = axisGroup.call(axis);
var domain = axisNodes.selectAll('.domain');
domain.attr({
    fill: 'none',
    'stroke-width': 1,
    stroke: 'black'
});
var ticks = axisNodes.selectAll('.tick line');
ticks.attr({
    fill: 'none',
    'stroke-width': 1,
    stroke: 'black'
});
```

The first change is that we create a group, represented by the variable `axisGroup`, to hold the axis that is generated. This will be used so that we can select the SVG elements in the axis representing the ticks and the axis line, and change their styles.

> It's good practice to always put the axes in a group. This facilitates style changes like the one we are performing in this example. Moreover, it is almost always the case that the axis needs to be translated into a specific position in the visualization. An axis itself cannot be translated, so placing it in a group element and then transforming the group accomplishes this task.

Secondly, the code captures the nodes that result from the generation of the axis in the `axisNodes` variable. Using `axisNode`, we can then perform two more selections to find specific elements in the axis: one for the element with the `domain` class, and the other for the line elements with the `line` class. Using the results of each of these two selections, the code then sets the `fill`, `stroke`, and `stroke-width` properties to make them all one pixel thick black lines.

Changing the axis orientation

D3.js axes can be rendered into four different orientations using the `.orient()` function on the axis, passing it the name of the orientation that is desired. The following table shows the orientation names that can be used:

`'top'`	Horizontal axis, with ticks and labels above the axis line.
`'bottom'`	Horizontal axis, with ticks and labels below the axis line (default)
`'left'`	Vertical axis, with ticks and labels to the left of the axis line
`'right'`	Vertical axis, with ticks and labels to the right of the axis line

Essentially, each of these relate to one of the four sides of a graph, such as the margins that were covered earlier. There is no effect of this function on the location of the axis in the visual (we have to do that ourselves). Instead, it decides whether the axis line is horizontal or vertical, and also if the labels are on the top or bottom of a horizontal axis or to the left or right of a vertical axis.

To demonstrate this, we will quickly inspect the top, right, and left orientations. Open the following link for an example of a top axis:

bl.ock (4.6): `http://bl.ocks.org/d3byex/8791783ee37ab76a8517`

There are two small modifications from the previous example. The primary change is that when we create the axis, we make a call to .orient('top'):

```
var axis = d3.svg.axis()
    .orient('top')
    .scale(scale);
```

The second change is that we need to translate the axis down the *Y* axis. We do this using the following statement:

```
axisGroup.attr('transform', 'translate(0,50)');
```

The result of the preceding example is as follows:

The orientation has moved the label and ticks to the top of the axis line instead of below.

The need for a transform is perhaps a little more subtle. If the axis was not transformed, all that we would see in the result is a single black line at the top of the rendering. This is because the positioning of an axis is relative to the path rendering the axis line. In this case, the line would be at $y = 0$, and the ticks and text would be clipped as they are above the line and not visible.

Now open the code for the following example, which renders a right-oriented axis. We will not examine the code, as it is a single simple change of calling .orient('right').

[bl.ock (4.7): http://goo.gl/H16kEo]

The result of the preceding code is the following:

```
┌ 0
├ 20
├ 40
├ 60
├ 80
├ 100
├ 120
├ 140
├ 160
├ 180
├ 200
```

The following example demonstrates a left-oriented axis. This is again a simple change of the parameter to .orient(). Additionally, the code also translates the axis to the right a bit, as the the ticks and labels would be clipped off the left.

bl.ock (4.8): http://goo.gl/CNEFyV

And the results are as follows:

```
  0
 20
 40
 60
 80
100
120
140
160
180
200
```

Inverting the labels on an axis

We want to place a left axis on our bar chart, essentially the output of example *4.8*. But if you examine the axis. you will notice that the labels are increasing from the top to the bottom. Our graph represents **0** at the bottom with values increasing upwards. This axis will not be appropriate for our graph.

This inversion of labels is a very simple change to the code. Open the following example:

bl.ock (4.9): http://goo.gl/wsm9Ab

The code is identical to example *4.8* except for one change.

```
var scale = d3.scale
    .linear()
    .domain([maxValue, 0])
    .range([0, maxValue]);
```

We change the order of the values passed to the domain, which will essentially reverse the order of the labels. This gives us the following result:

The labels have been reversed into the order that we desire. Note now that the label 0 is clipped at the bottom. We will fix this in our next example when we combine the axis with the bar graph.

Adding the axis to the graph

We now have everything that we need to create a bar graph with an axis. Essentially, we only need to combine the code from example 4.3 with the axis code from example 4.9. The following example does exactly this:

bl.ock (4.10): http://goo.gl/MsKhUk

And the result is the following graph, which is exactly what we wanted:

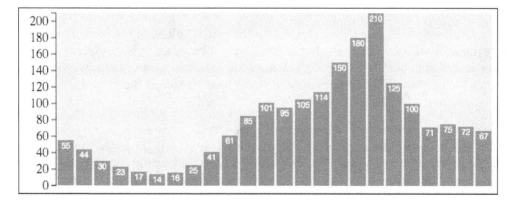

The code in this example is identical to the one in example 4.3 up to the point where we create the group to contain the axis:

```
var leftAxisGroup = svg.append('g');
var axisPadding = 3;
leftAxisGroup.attr({
    transform: 'translate(' + (margin.left - axisPadding) + ','
                            + margin.top + ')' });
```

The change here is the translation of the axis along the X axis by the width of the left margin, and down the Y axis by the size of the top margin. For aesthetics, the code simply renders the axis with three pixels of padding.

 Also note that since we have margin space at the bottom, the **0** label is no longer truncated.

Summary

In this chapter, you extended your knowledge of using D3 to create a bar graph from a collection of integers. You learned how to position and size each element of the graph according to its data, and how to position groups of data that contain multiple visuals representing a single bar—specifically, how to add a label that represents the value of the underlying datum at the top of a bar.

We then examined the facilities in D3.js for creating axes. We introduced the concept of a scale, which is an important facet of implementing axes. We further examined the different orientations available for an axis, and how to invert the order of the labels on an axis. Finally, we combined the axis and the bar graph together into an effective visualization of the data.

As great as our bar chart looks in this example, we will still have several issues. The overall size of the graph was related to the actual values of the data. This was convenient for demonstrating the construction of a bar graph visualization, but what if the values are not integers, or if the values are extremely small or large? We might not see the bars at all, or the bars may be so large as to exceed the size of the main SVG element.

In the next chapter, we will address these issues by learning more about scales. Scales will provide an exceptionally easy means of mapping data into the physical dimensions of a visualization. You will also learn about loading data from external sources, and about working with data that is more complex in structure than simple integers.

5
Using Data and Scales

In *Chapter 4, Creating a Bar Graph*, you learned how to create a bar graph that was based upon a sequence of integers that were statically coded within the application. Although the resulting graph looks quite nice, there are several issues with the way the data is provided and rendered.

One of the issues is that the data is hard-coded within the application. Almost invariably, we are going to load the data from an external source. D3.js provides a rich set of functionalities for loading data from sources over the web, and which is represented in different formats. In this chapter, you will learn to use D3.js for loading data from the web in JSON, CSV, and TSV formats.

A second issue with the data in the example given in the previous chapter was that it was simply an array of integers. Data will often be represented as collections of objects with multiple properties, many of which we do not need for our visualization. They are also often represented as strings instead of numeric values. In this chapter, you will learn how to select just the data that you want and to convert it to the desired data type.

Yet another issue in our previous bar graph was that we assumed that the values represented in the data had a direct mapping to the pixels in the visualization. This is normally not the case, and we need to scale the data into the size of our rendering in the browser. This can be easily accomplished using scales, which we already examined relative to axes, and now we will apply them to data.

One last issue in the previous example was that our code for calculating the size and positions of the bars was performed manually. Bar graphs are common enough in D3.js applications, and there are built-in functions that can do this for us automatically. We will examine using these to simplify our code.

So let's jump in. In this chapter, we will specifically cover the following topics:

- Loading data in JSON, TSV, or CSV formats from the Web
- Extracting fields from objects using the `.map()` function
- Converting string values into their representative numeric data types
- Using linear scales for transforming continuous values
- Using ordinal scales for mapping discrete data
- Using bands for calculating the size and position of our bars
- Applying what we've learned to date for creating a rich bar graph using real data

Data

Data is the core of creating a data visualization. Almost every visual item created in D3 will need to be bound to a piece of data. This data can come from a number of sources. It can be explicitly coded in the visualization, loaded from an external source, or result from manipulation or calculation from other data.

Most data used to create a D3.js visualization is either obtained from a file or a web service or URL. This data is often in one of many formats such as JSON, XML, **CSV (Comma Separated Values)**, and **TSV (Tab Separated Values)**. We will need to convert the data in these formats into JavaScript objects, and D3.js provides us with convenient functions for doing this.

Loading data with D3.js

D3.js provides a number of helper functions to load data from outside the browser as well as to simultaneously convert it into JavaScript objects. Probably, the most common data formats that you may come across and which we will cover are:

- JSON
- TSV
- CSV

You may have noticed that I have omitted XML from the list in our examples. D3.js does have functions to load XML, but unlike with JSON, TSV and CSV, the results of the load are not converted automatically into JavaScript objects, and require additional manipulation using the JavaScript XML/DOM facilities. XML will be considered out of scope for this text as most of the scenarios you will currently come across will be handled with these three formats, if not solely by JSON, which has become almost the ubiquitous data format for the Web.

To demonstrate working with all these formats of data, we will examine a dataset that I have put together and placed in a GitHub that represents the viewership of the episodes of Season 5 of AMC's *The Walking Dead*.

 This GitHub was built manually using data on `https://en.wikipedia.org/wiki/The_Walking_Dead_(season_5)`.

Loading JSON data

Data in the **JavaScript Object Notation (JSON)** format is convenient for conversion into JavaScript objects. It is a very flexible format which supports named properties as well as hierarchical data.

The JSON data for this example is stored in GitHub and is available at `https://gist.githubusercontent.com/d3byex/e5ce6526ba2208014379/raw/8fefb14cc18f0440dc00248f23cbf6aec80dcc13/walking_dead_s5.json`.

 The URL is a little unwieldy. You can go directly to the gist with all three versions of this data at `https://goo.gl/OfD1hc`.

Clicking on the link will display the data in the browser. This file contains an array of JavaScript objects, each of which has six properties and represents an individual episode of the program. The first two objects are the following:

```
[
{
  "Season": 5,
  "Episode":  1,
  "SeriesNumber": 52,
  "Title": "No Sanctuary",
  "FirstAirDate": "10-12-2014",
  "USViewers": 17290000
},
```

```
{
    "Season": 5,
    "Episode":  2,
    "SeriesNumber": 53,
    "Title": "Strangers",
    "FirstAirDate": "10-19-2014",
    "USViewers": 15140000
},
...
]
```

This data can be loaded into our D3.js application using the d3.json() function. This function, like many others in D3.js, performs asynchronously. It takes two parameters: the URL of the data to load, and a callback function that is called when the data has been loaded.

The following example demonstrates loading this data and displaying the first item in the array.

bl.ock (5.1): http://goo.gl/Qe63wH

The main portion of the code that loads the data is as follows:

```
var url = "https://gist.githubusercontent.com/d3byex/
e5ce6526ba2208014379/raw/8fefb14cc18f0440dc00248f23cbf6aec80dcc13/
walking_dead_s5.json";
d3.json(url, function (error, data) {
    console.log(data[0]);
});
console.log("Data in D3.js is loaded asynchronously");
```

There is no visible output from this example, but the output is written to the JavaScript console:

```
"Data in D3.js is loaded asynchronously"
[object Object] {
    Episode: 1,
    FirstAirDate: "10-12-2014",
    Season: 5,
    SeriesNumber: 52,
    Title: "No Sanctuary",
    USViewers: 17290000
}
```

Note that the loading of data in D3.js is performed asynchronously. The output from the `console.log()` call shows that the data is loaded asynchronously and is executed first. Later, when the data is loaded, we see the output from the second call to `console.log()`.

The callback function itself has two parameters. The first is a reference to an object representing an error if one occurs. In such a case, this variable will be non-null and contain details. Non-null means the data was loaded, and is represented by the data variable.

Loading TSV data

TSV is a type of data that you will come across if you do enough D3.js programming. In a TSV file, the values are separated by tab characters. Generally, the first line of the file is a tab-separated sequence of names for each of the values.

TSV files have the benefit of being less verbose than JSON files, and are often generated automatically by many systems that are not JavaScript based.

The episode data in the TSV format is available at `https://gist. githubusercontent.com/d3byex/e5ce6526ba2208014379/raw/8fefb14cc18f044 0dc00248f23cbf6aec80dcc13/walking_dead_s5.tsv`.

Clicking on the link, you will see the following in your browser:

```
Season Episode SeriesNumber Title FirstAirDate USViewers
5 1 52 No Sanctuary 10-12-2014 17290000
5 2 53 Strangers 10-19-2014 15140000
5 3 54 Four Walls and a Roof 10-26-2014 13800000
5 4 55 Slabtown 11-02-2014 14520000
5 5 56 Self Help 11-09-2014 13530000
5 6 57 Consumed 11-16-2014 14070000
5 7 58 Crossed 11-23-2014 13330000
5 8 59 Coda 11-30-2014 14810000
5 9 60 What Happened and What's Going On 02-08-2015 15640000
5 10 61 Them 02-15-2015 12270000
5 11 62 The Distance 02-22-2015 13440000
5 12 63 Remember 03-01-2015 14430000
5 13 64 Forget 03-08-2015 14530000
5 14 65 Spend 03-15-2015 13780000
5 15 66 Try 03-22-2015 13760000
5 16 67 Conquer 03-29-2015 15780000
```

We can load the data from this file using d3.tsv(). The following contains the code for the example:

bl.ock (5.2): http://goo.gl/nlq8jy

The code is identical to the JSON example except for the URL and the call to d3.json(). The output in the console is, however, different.

```
[object Object] {
    Episode: "1",
    FirstAirDate: "10-12-2014",
    Season: "5",
    SeriesNumber: "52",
    Title: "No Sanctuary",
    USViewers: "17290000"
}
```

Notice that the properties **Episode, Season, SeriesNumber**, and **USViewers** are now of type string instead of integer. TSV files do not have a means of implying the type like JSON does, so everything defaults to string. These will often need to be converted to another type, and we will examine that in the next section on mapping and data conversion.

Loading CSV data

CSV is a format similar to TSV except that instead of tab characters delimiting the fields, a comma is used. CSV is a fairly common format, common as output from spreadsheet applications, which is used for creating data to be consumed by other applications in many organizations.

The CSV version of the data is available at https://gist.githubusercontent.com/d3byex/e5ce6526ba2208014379/raw/8fefb14cc18f0440dc00248f23cbf6aec80dcc13/walking_dead_s5.csv.

Opening the link, you will see the following in your browser:

```
Season,Episode,SeriesNumber,Title,FirstAirDate,USViewers
5,1,52,No Sanctuary,10-12-2014,17290000
5,2,53,Strangers,10-19-2014,15140000
5,3,54,Four Walls and a Roof,10-26-2014,13800000
5,4,55,Slabtown,11-02-2014,14520000
5,5,56,Self Help,11-09-2014,13530000
```

```
5,6,57,Consumed,11-16-2014,14070000
5,7,58,Crossed,11-23-2014,13330000
5,8,59,Coda,11-30-2014,14810000
5,9,60,What Happened and What's Going On,02-08-2015,15640000
5,10,61,Them,02-15-2015,12270000
5,11,62,The Distance,02-22-2015,13440000
5,12,63,Remember,03-01-2015,14430000
5,13,64,Forget,03-08-2015,14530000
5,14,65,Spend,03-15-2015,13780000
5,15,66,Try,03-22-2015,13760000
5,16,67,Conquer,03-29-2015,15780000
```

The example for demonstrating the loading of the preceding data using d3.csv() is available at the following link:

bl.ock (5.3): http://goo.gl/JUX9CA

The result is identical to that of the TSV example in that all the fields are loaded as strings.

Mapping fields and converting strings to numbers

We are going to use this data (in its CSV source) to render a bar graph that shows us the comparison of the viewership levels for each episode. If we are to use these fields as-is for creating the bar graph, those values will be interpreted incorrectly as their types are strings instead of numbers, and our resulting graph will be incorrect.

Additionally, for the purpose of creating a bar chart showing viewership, we don't need the properties and can omit the Season, SeriesNumber, and FirstAirDate fields. It's not a real issue with this dataset, but sometimes, the data can have hundreds of columns and billions of rows, so it will be more efficient to extract only the necessary properties to help save memory.

These can be accomplished in a naive manner using a for loop, copying the desired fields into a new JavaScript object, and using one of the parse functions to convert the data. D3.js gives us a better way, a functional way, to perform this task.

D3.js provides us with the a .map() function that can be used on an array, which will apply a function to each of the array's items. This function returns a JavaScript object, and D3.js collects all these objects and returns them in an array. This gives us a simple way of selecting just the properties that we want and to convert the data, all in a single statement.

To demonstrate this in action, open the example given at the following link:

 bl.ock (5.4): `http://goo.gl/ex2e8C`

The important portion of the code is the call to `data.map()`:

```
var mappedAndConverted = data.map(function(d) {
    return {
        Episode: +d.Episode,
        USViewers: +d.USViewers,
        Title: d.Title
    };
});
console.log(mappedAndConverted);
```

The function that is passed to the .map() returns a new JavaScript object for each item in the array data. This new object consists of only the three specified properties. These objects are all collected by .map() and stored in the mappedAndConverted variable.

The following code shows the first two objects in the new array:

```
[[object Object] {
  Episode: 1,
  Title: "No Sanctuary",
  USViewers: 17290000
}, [object Object] {
  Episode: 2,
  Title: "Strangers",
  USViewers: 15140000
},
```

Note that Episode and USViewers are now numeric values. This is accomplished by applying the unary + operator, which will convert a string to its appropriate numeric type.

Scales

Scales are functions provided by D3.js that map a set of values to another set of values. The input set of values is referred to as the domain, and the output is the range. The basic reason for the existence of scales is to prevent us from coding loops, and doing a lot of math to make these conversions happen. This is a very useful thing.

There are three general categories of scales: quantitative, ordinal, and time-scale. Within each category of scale, D3.js provides a number of concrete implementations that exist for accomplishing a specific type of mapping data useful for data visualization.

Covering examples of every type of scale would consume more space than is available in this book, and at the same time become tedious to read. We will examine several common scales that are used – kind of the 80/20 rule, where the few we cover here will be used most of the time you use scales.

Linear scales

Linear scales are a type of quantitative scale that are arguably the most commonly used ones. The mapping performed is linear in that the output range is calculated using a linear function of the input domain.

A good example of using a linear scale is the scenario with our *The Walking Dead* viewership data. We need to draw bars from this data; but if we use the code that we used earlier in the book, our bars will be extremely tall since that code has a one to one mapping between the value and the pixels.

Let's assume that our area for the bars on the graph has a height of 400 pixels. We would like to map the lowest viewership value to a bar that is 100 pixels tall, and map the largest viewership value to 400. The following example performs this task:

bl.ock (5.5): `http://goo.gl/dgg0zf`

The code starts, as with the CSV example, by loading that data and mapping/ converting it. The next task is to determine the minimum and maximum viewership values:

```
var viewership = mappedAndConverted.map(function (d) {
    return d.USViewers;
});
var minViewership = d3.min(viewership);
var maxViewership = d3.max(viewership);
```

Next, we define several variables representing the minimum and maximum height that we would like for the bars:

```
var minBarHeight = 100, maxBarHeight = 400;
```

The scale is then created as follows:

```
var yScale = d3.scale
    .linear()
    .domain([minViewership, maxViewership])
    .range([minBarHeight, maxBarHeight]);
```

We can now use the yScale object as though it is a function. The following will log the results of scaling the minimum and maximum viewership values:

```
console.log(minViewership + " -> " + yScale(minViewership));
console.log(maxViewership + " -> " + yScale(maxViewership));
```

Examining the console output, we can see that the scaling resulted in the expected values:

```
"12270000 -> 100"
"17290000 -> 400"
```

Ordinal scales

Ordinal scales are, in a way, similar to dictionary objects. The values in the domain and range are discrete. There must be an entry in the range for every unique input value, and that value must have a mapping to a single value in the range.

There are several common uses for ordinal scales, and we will examine four common uses that we will use throughout the remainder of this book.

Mapping color strings to codes

Open the following link for an example of an ordinal scale. This example does not use the data from *The Walking Dead*, and simply demonstrates the mapping of string literals representing primary colors into the corresponding color codes.

bl.ock (5.6): http://goo.gl/DezcUN

The scale is created as follows:

```
var colorScale = d3.scale.ordinal()
    .domain(['red', 'green', 'blue'])
    .range(['#ff0000', '#00ff00', '#0000ff']);
```

We can now pass any of the range values to the `colorScale`, as demonstrated with the following:

```
console.log(colorScale('red'),
    colorsScale('green'),
    colorScale('blue'));
```

Examining the console output, we can see the results of this mapping as follows:

```
"#ff0000"
"#00ff00"
"#0000ff"
```

Mapping integers to color scales

D3.js comes with several special built-in scales that are referred to as **categorical** scales. It sounds like a fancy term, but they are simply mappings of a set of integers to unique colors (unique within that scale).

These are useful when you have a set of sequential 0-based integer keys in your data, and you want to use a unique color for each, but you do not want to manually create all the mappings (like we did for the three strings in the previous example).

Open the following link for an example of using a 10 color categorical scale:

bl.ock (5.7): `http://goo.gl/RSW9Qa`

The preceding example renders 10 adjacent rectangles, each with a unique color from a `category10()` color scale. You will see this in your browser when executing this example.

The example starts by creating an array of 10 integers from 0 to 9.

```
var data = d3.range(0, 9);
```

The scale is created next:

```
var colorScale = d3.scale.category10();
```

Now we can bind the integers to the rectangles, and set the fill for each by passing the value to the `colorScale` function:

```
var svg = d3.select('body')
    .append('svg')
    .attr({width: 200, height: 20});

svg.selectAll('rect')
    .data(data)
    .enter()
    .append('rect')
    .attr({
        fill: function(d) { return colorScale(d); },
        x: function(d, i) { return i * 20 },
        width: 20,
        height: 20
    });
```

D3.js provides four sets of categorical color scales that can be used depending upon your scenario. You can take a look at them on the D3.js documentation page at `https://github.com/mbostock/d3/wiki/Ordinal-Scales`.

The ordinal scale using rangeBands

In *Chapter 4, Creating a Bar Graph*, when we drew the graph we calculated the positions of the bars based upon a fixed bar size and padding. This is actually a very inflexible means of accomplishing this task. D3.js gives us a special scale that we can use, given the domain values and essentially a width, that will tell us the start and end values for each bar such that all the bars fit perfectly within the range!

Let's take a look using this special scale with the following example:

bl.ock (5.8): `http://goo.gl/OG3g7S`

This example creates a simple ordinal scale specifying the range using the
`.rangeBands()` function instead of `.range()`. The entire code of the example is as
follows:

```
var bands = d3.scale.ordinal()
    .domain([0, 1, 2])
    .rangeBands([0, 100]);
console.log(bands.range());
console.log(bands.rangeBand());
```

The `.range()` function will return an array with values representing the
extents of an equal number of evenly-spaced divisions of the range specified to
`.rangeBands()`. In this case, the width of the range is `100`, and there are three items
specified in the domain; hence, the result is the following:

```
[0, 33.333333333333336, 66.66666666666667]
```

Technically, this result is the values that represent the start of each band. The width
of each band can be found using the `.rangeBand()` function, in this case returning
the following:

```
33.333333333333336
```

This width may seem simplistic. Why have this function if we can just calculate the
difference between two adjacent values in the result of `.range()`? To demonstrate,
let's look at a slight modification of this example, available at the following link.

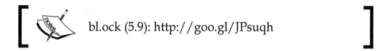

bl.ock (5.9): http://goo.gl/JPsuqh

This makes one modification to the call to `.rangeBands()`, adding an additional
parameter that specifies the padding that should exist between the bars:

```
var bands = d3.scale.ordinal()
    .domain([0, 1, 2])
    .rangeRoundBands([0, 100], 0.1);
```

The output differs slightly due to the addition of padding between the bands:

```
[3.2258064516129035, 35.483870967741936, 67.74193548387096]
29.032258064516128
```

The width of each band is now 29.03, with a padding of 3.23 between bands
(including on the outside of the two outer bands).

The value for padding is a value between 0.0 (the default, and which results in a padding of 0) and 1.0, resulting in bands of width 0.0. A value of 0.5 makes the padding the same width as each band.

Visualizing The Walking Dead viewership

Now we pull everything from the chapter together to render a bar graph of the viewership across all the episodes of *The Walking Dead*:

bl.ock (5.10): `http://goo.gl/T8d6OU`

The output of the preceding example is as follows:

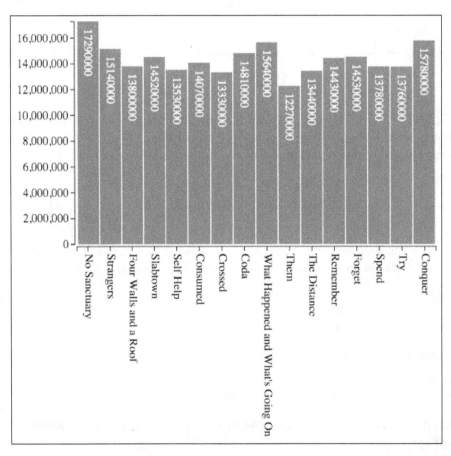

Now let's step through how this is created. After loading the data from the JSON file, the first thing that is performed is the extraction of the `USViewership` values and the determining of the maximum value:

```
var viewership = data.map(function (d) {
    return d.USViewers;
});

var maxViewers = d3.max(viewership);
```

Then various variables, which represent various metrics for the graph, and the main SVG element are created:

```
var margin = { top: 10, right: 10, bottom: 260, left: 85 };

var graphWidth = 500, graphHeight = 300;

var totalWidth = graphWidth + margin.left + margin.right;
var totalHeight = graphHeight + margin.top + margin.bottom;

var axisPadding = 3;

var svg = d3.select('body')
    .append('svg')
    .attr({ width: totalWidth, height: totalHeight });
```

The container for holding the bars is created next:

```
var mainGroup = svg
    .append('g')
    .attr('transform', 'translate(' + margin.left + ',' +
                                margin.top + ")");
```

Now we create an ordinal scale for the bars using `.rangeBands()`. We will use this to calculate the bar position and padding:

```
var bands = d3.scale.ordinal()
    .domain(viewership)
    .rangeBands([0, graphWidth], 0.05);
```

We also require a scale to calculate the height of each bar:

```
var yScale = d3.scale
    .linear()
    .domain([0, maxViewers])
    .range([0, graphHeight]);
```

The following function is used by the selection that creates the bars to position each of them:

```
function translator(d, i) {
    return "translate(" + bands.range()[i] + "," +
                        (graphHeight - yScale(d)) + ")";
}
```

Now we create the groups for the content of each bar:

```
var barGroup = mainGroup.selectAll('g')
    .data(viewership)
    .enter()
    .append('g')
    .attr('transform', translator);
```

Next we append the rectangle for the bar:

```
barGroup.append('rect')
    .attr({
        fill: 'steelblue',
        width: bands.rangeBand(),
        height: function(d) { return yScale(d); }
    });
```

And then add a label to the bar to show the exact viewership value:

```
barGroup.append('text')
    .text(function(d) { return d; })
    .style('text-anchor', 'start')
    .attr({
        dx: 10,
        dy: -10,
        transform: 'rotate(90)',
        fill: 'white'
    });
```

The bars are now complete, so we move on to creating both the axes. We start with the left axis:

```
var leftAxisGroup = svg.append('g');
leftAxisGroup.attr({
    transform: 'translate(' + (margin.left - axisPadding) + ',' +
                            margin.top + ')'
});

var yAxisScale = d3.scale
```

```
        .linear()
        .domain([maxViewers, 0])
        .range([0, graphHeight]);

    var leftAxis = d3.svg.axis()
        .orient('left')
        .scale(yAxisScale);
    var leftAxisNodes = leftAxisGroup.call(leftAxis);
    styleAxisNodes(leftAxisNodes);
```

And now create a bottom axis which displays the titles:

```
    var titles = data.map(function(d) { return d.Title; });
    var bottomAxisScale = d3.scale.ordinal()
        .domain(titles)
        .rangeBands([axisPadding, graphWidth + axisPadding]);

    var bottomAxis = d3.svg
        .axis()
        .scale(bottomAxisScale)
        .orient("bottom");

    var bottomAxisX = margin.left - axisPadding;
    var bottomAxisY = totalHeight - margin.bottom + axisPadding;

    var bottomAxisGroup = svg.append("g")
        .attr({ transform: 'translate(' + bottomAxisX + ',' + bottomAxisY
    + ')' });

    var bottomAxisNodes = bottomAxisGroup.call(bottomAxis);
    styleAxisNodes(bottomAxisNodes);

    bottomAxisNodes.selectAll("text")
        .style('text-anchor', 'start')
        .attr({
            dx: 10,
            dy: -5,
            transform: 'rotate(90)'
    });
```

The following function is reusable code for styling the axes:

```
    function styleAxisNodes(axisNodes) {
        axisNodes.selectAll('.domain')
            .attr({
                fill: 'none',
```

```
                    'stroke-width': 1,
                    stroke: 'black'
             });
        axisNodes.selectAll('.tick line')
             .attr({
                 fill: 'none',
                 'stroke-width': 1,
                 stroke: 'black'
             });
    }
```

Summary

In this chapter, you learned how to load data from the web and use it as the basis for a bar graph. We started with loading data in the JSON, CSV, and TSV formats. You learned how to use the `.map()` function to extract just the values that you desire from this data, and examined the issues and solutions needed for converting string values into numeric values.

Next we covered scales in some more detail, and looked at several examples of the ways to use scales for mapping data from one range of values to another as well as to map discrete values such as color names to color codes. We covered categorical scales, a means of mapping integer values into predefined color maps, and a concept that we will use frequently in our examples. Our examination of scales ended with a demonstration of using `.rangeBands()`, and how it can help us size and place bars within a predefined area.

We closed the chapter by combining all of these concepts together into, what is up to this point, our best example of generating a bar chart. This demonstrated loading the data, using multiple scales for both data and axes, and using `.rangeBands()` to determine the placement of the bars, as well as using not only a vertical but also a horizontal axis.

In the next chapter, we will branch out of bar graphs into another type of data visualization—scatter (and bubble) plots.

6

Creating Scatter and Bubble Plots

In this chapter, we extend our examples of using D3.js for plotting data to explain how to create scatter and bubble plots. Scatter and bubble plots visualize multivariate data, as compared to univariate data that is visualized by bar charts. Multivariate data consists of two or more variables, and scatter plots allow us to visualize two variable, and bubble plots extend this to three or four variables.

We will begin by first creating a simple scatter plot with fixed symbols, based upon stock correlation data. We start with using solid circles for symbols, and will progress through several enhancements including the use of color, outlines, and opacity. We will wrap up scatter plots with an example of multiple, overlying sets of data, each using different symbols and colors.

When we've finished examining the of creation of a bubble plot, we will extend that example to change the size of the points based upon the data, and then to color the points based upon categorical information. This last example will demonstrate how we can visualize four different variables within a single visualization, and how the use of visuals can help us derive meaning from the underlying information.

Specifically, in this chapter we will cover the following topics:

- Creating a basic scatter plot using fixed-sized and solid points
- Using outlines instead of solid fills to make the plot more legible
- Adding gridlines to help determine the location of points
- Extending the scatter plot code to create bubble plots

Creating scatter plots

Scatter plots consist of two axes, one for each variable. Each axis can be based on continuous or categorical variables. For each measurement (a **measurement** being the paired combination of X and Y values), a symbol is placed on the plot at the specified location. The end result is a plot that allows the person viewing it to determine how much one variable is affected by the other.

Underpinning our first few examples will be a data set that represents the correlation between the AAPL and MSFT stocks on a daily basis for the year 2014. For purposes of creating a scatter plot, the meaning of this data is not important—it is just that it represents two dimensional data, where the value for each stock represents a location on the respective axis.

The data for this example is available at `https://goo.gl/BZkC8B`.

Opening this link in the browser, you will see the following as the first few lines of the data:

```
Date,AAPL,MSFT
2014-01-02,-0.01406,-0.00668
2014-01-03,-0.02197,-0.00673
2014-01-06,0.00545,-0.02113
2014-01-07,-0.00715,0.00775
2014-01-08,0.00633,-0.01785
2014-01-09,-0.01277,-0.00643
2014-01-10,-0.00667,0.01435
2014-01-13,0.00524,-0.02941
2014-01-14,0.0199,0.02287
2014-01-15,0.02008,0.02739
```

Plotting points

Our first example will demonstrate the process of drawing points in a scatter plot. To keep it simple, it forgoes the axes and other stylistic elements (these will be added in the next example).

The example is available at the following location:

[bl.ock (6.1): `http://goo.gl/Uv6aSj`]

The resulting plot is seen in the following image:

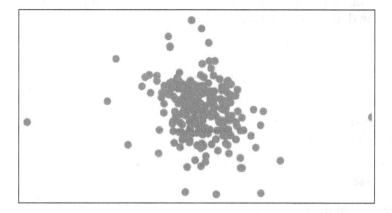

Now let's examine how this is created. The example starts by loading the data:

```
var url = "https://gist.githubusercontent.com/
d3byex/520e6dcb30e673c149cc/raw/432623f00f6740021bdc13141612ac0b619
6b022/corr_aapl_msft.csv";
d3.csv(url, function (error, rawData) {
```

 The entire URL has to be specified, as apparently, the data load functions do not follow redirects.

We need to convert the properties AAPL and MSFT from strings to numbers. We do this by creating a new array of objects with x and y properties, with AAPL mapped into x and MSFT into y, which also converts the data type:

```
var data = rawData.map(function(d) {
    return { X: +d.AAPL, Y: +d.MSFT }
});
```

To effectively scale a scatter plot, we need to know the extents of the data in both the x and y series:

```
var xExtents = d3.extent(data, function(d) { return d.X; });
var yExtents = d3.extent(data, function(d) { return d.Y; });
```

These values will help us create the scales that are required for both dimensions of the graph. This plot will actually use the maximum absolute value of these four extents. We can determine this value with the following:

```
var maxExtent = d3.max(
    xExtents.concat(yExtents),
    function(d) { return Math.abs(d);
});
```

We are now ready to create the properties of the graph, including its width, height, and the size of the radius for the circles that will represent the points:

```
var graphWidth = 400, graphHeight = 400;
var radius = 5;
```

Now we have all of the information required to create the scale needed to map the data into the locations in the rendering:

```
var scale = d3.scale.linear()
    .domain([-maxExtent, maxExtent])
    .range([0, graphWidth]);
```

This example (and those in the remainder of this chapter) scale the data such that the domain is the negative and positive of the absolute values of the extents. In simple terms, this scale ensures that when rendering into a square canvas, all points are visible and any specific distance along the X dimension represents an identical change in the value of the data as the distance along the Y dimension.

The rendering begins with the creation of the main SVG element:

```
var svg = d3.select('body')
    .append('svg')
    .attr('width', graphWidth)
    .attr('height', graphHeight);
```

Finally, we create a circle of the specified radius to represent each point:

```
svg.selectAll('circle')
    .data(data)
    .enter()
    .append('circle')
    .attr({
        cx: function(d) { return xScale(d.AAPL); },
        cy: function(d) { return yScale(d.MSFT); },
        r: radius,
```

```
        fill: 'steelblue'
      });
}); // closing the call to d3.csv
```

Congratulations, you have created your first scatter plot!

Sprucing up the scatter plot

There are several issues with the plot in the previous example. First, notice that there is a circle that is clipped towards the right boundary. With the code as it is, one point, the one at the maximum extent, will have half of its area clipped. This can easily be resolved by including margins that are at least half of the radius of the circles.

Another issue is that there are a lot of circles that overlap, confusing the visual understanding of the data. A common means of addressing this issue in scatter plots is not to use a solid fill in the circles, and simply use an outline instead.

A final issue, which is really just a decision made to keep the previous example simple, is not to have any axes. The example at the following link addresses each of these concerns:

bl.ock (6.2): http://goo.gl/4T1aGZ

The preceding example has the following output:

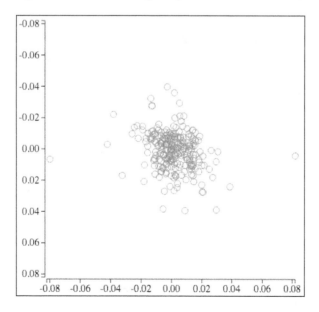

This result is a much more effective scatter plot. We can make sense of the previously obscured points, and the axes give us a sense of the values at each point.

The changes to the code are relatively minor. Besides adding axes by using the code that we have seen in other examples (including grouping groups for the various main elements), and sizing the main SVG element to account for those axes, the only change is in the way the circles are created:

```
graphGroup.selectAll('circle')
    .data(data)
    .enter()
    .append('circle')
    .attr({
        cx: function(d) { return scale(d.X); },
        cy: function(d) { return scale(d.Y); },
        r: radius,
        fill: 'none',
        stroke: 'steelblue'
    });
```

Adding gridlines

Our scatter plot would be more effective if it had gridlines. The way in which we add gridlines to a chart in D3.js is actually a little trick: gridlines are actually the ticks of an axis, the ticks being the width or height of the graphic with both the labels and main line of the axis hidden.

To add gridlines to our plot, we will create two additional axes. The horizontal gridlines will be rendered by creating a left-oriented axis positioned in the right margin. We will set the labels on this axis to be empty and the line of the axis to be hidden. The ticks are then sized to extend all the way back to the other axis in the left margin. We will perform a similar process to create the vertical gridlines except with a bottom axis placed in the top margin.

[bl.ock (6.3): `http://goo.gl/ZmrY4H`]

And the resulting graph is shown in the following image:

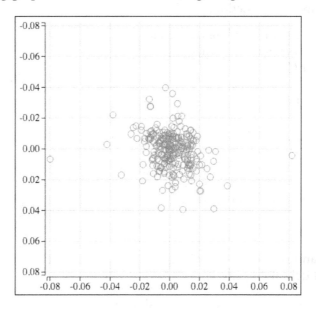

The only difference from the previous examples are the several lines for creating these new axes and a function to style them:

```
var yGridlinesAxis = d3.svg.axis().scale(scale).orient("left");
var yGridlineNodes = svg.append('g')
    .attr('transform', 'translate(' + (margins.left + graphWidth)
                    + ',' + margins.top + ')')
    .call(yGridlinesAxis
        .tickSize(graphWidth + axisPadding, 0, 0)
        .tickFormat(""));
styleGridlineNodes(yGridlineNodes);
```

The code begins with creating a left-oriented axis, and then renders it in a group which is translated to the right margin.

Instead of simply passing the axis object to .call(), we first call two of its functions. The first, .tickSize(), sets the size of the ticks to stretch across the entire area where the points will be rendered. Calling .tickFormat("") informs the axis that the labels should be empty.

Now we just need to perform a little styling on the axis. This is performed by the `styleGridLineNodes()` function:

```
function styleGridlineNodes(axisNodes) {
    axisNodes.selectAll('.domain')
        .attr({
            fill: 'none',
            stroke: 'none'
        });
    axisNodes.selectAll('.tick line')
        .attr({
            fill: 'none',
            'stroke-width': 1,
            stroke: 'lightgray'
        });
}
```

This sets the fill and stroke of the main line of the axis so that it is not visible. It then makes the actual ticks light gray.

The vertical gridlines are then created by a similar process:

```
var xGridlinesAxis = d3.svg.axis().scale(scale).orient("bottom");
var xGridlineNodes = svg.append('g')
    .attr('transform', 'translate(' + margins.left + ',' +
            (totalHeight - margins.bottom + axisPadding) + ')')
    .call(xGridlinesAxis
        .tickSize(-graphWidth - axisPadding, 0, 0)
        .tickFormat(""));
styleGridlineNodes(xGridlineNodes);
```

A final point about this process is the sequence of the renderings: gridlines, then axes, then the points. This ensures that each of these appear on top of the others. It is most important for the points to be on top of the gridlines and axes, but the gridlines also being behind the visible axes is good practice. It gives you a little wiggle room to be a few pixels long on the gridlines.

Creating a bubble plot

Bubble plots help us to visualize three or four dimensions of data. Each datum in a bubble plot consists not only of two values used to plot against the X and Y axes, but also one or two additional values which are commonly represented by different size symbols and/or colors.

To demonstrate a bubble plot, the following image shows the result of our example:

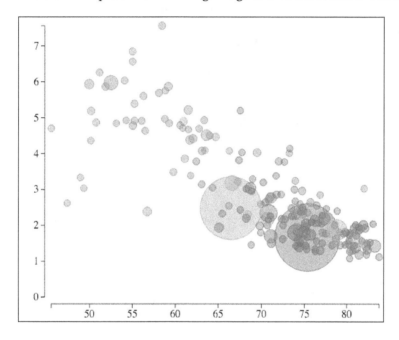

The data behind this chart is a data set that was pulled together from three different datasets from the World Bank. This data correlates life expectancy at birth relative to the fertility rate for all the countries in the World Bank data for the year 2013.

This chart plots age along the X axis and the birth rate along the Y axis. The relative population of a country is represented by the size of the circle, and the color of the circle represents the economic region of the country as categorized by the World Bank.

We won't dive deeply into this data. It is available at `https://goo.gl/K3yuuy`.

The first few lines of the data are the following:

```
CountryCode,CountryName,LifeExp,FertRate,Population,Region
ABW,Aruba,75.33217073,1.673,102911,Latin America & Caribbean
AFG,Afghanistan,60.93141463,4.9,30551674,South Asia
```

If you want to check out the original data, you can use the following links:

- Life expectancy (in years) at birth: `http://data.worldbank.org/indicator/SP.DYN.LE00.IN`
- Fertility rate: `http://data.worldbank.org/indicator/SP.DYN.TFRT.IN`
- Total population: `http://data.worldbank.org/indicator/SP.POP.TOTL`

The code for the example is available at the following link:

bl.ock (6.4): `http://goo.gl/KQJceE`

The example starts with the loading of data and converting the data types:

```
var url = "https://gist.githubusercontent.com/
d3byex/30231953acaa9433a46f/raw/6c7eb1c562de92bdf8d0cd99c6912048161c18
7e/fert_pop_exp.csv";
    var data = rawData.map(function(d) {
        return {
            CountryCode: d.CountryCode,
            CountryName: d.CountryName,
            LifeExp: +d.LifeExp,
            FertRate: +d.FertRate,
            Population: +d.Population,
            Region: d.Region
        }
    });
```

Now we define several variables for defining the minimum and maximum bubble size and the margins, which we will set to be half of the radius of the largest bubble:

```
var minBubbleSize = 5, maxBubbleSize = 50;
var margin = { left: maxBubbleSize/2, top: maxBubbleSize/2,
               bottom: maxBubbleSize/2, right: maxBubbleSize/2
};
```

This particular plot requires three linear scales and one ordinal scale based upon the following four series of data:

```
var lifeExpectancy = data.map(function(d) { return d.LifeExp; });
var fertilityRate = data.map(function(d) { return d.FertRate; });
var population = data.map(function(d) { return d.Population; });
var regions = data.map(function(d) { return d.Region; });
```

The scale for the X axis will vary from the minimum to the maximum life expectancy:

```
var xScale = d3.scale.linear()
    .domain([d3.min(lifeExpectancy), d3.max(lifeExpectancy)])
    .range([0, graphWidth]);
```

The Y axis will range from the maximum fertility rate at the top to 0 at the bottom:

```
var yScale = d3.scale.linear()
    .domain([d3.max(fertilityRate), 0])
    .range([0, graphHeight]);
```

The size of each bubble represents the population, and will range in radius from the minimum to the maximum values configured earlier:

```
var popScale = d3.scale.linear()
    .domain(d3.extent(population))
    .range([minBubbleSize, maxBubbleSize]);
```

Each bubble will be colored based upon the value of the region. To do this, we set up a mapping between each of the unique names of the regions and a 10-color categorical scale:

```
var uniqueRegions = d3.set(regions).values();
var regionColorMap = d3.scale.ordinal()
    .domain(uniqueRegions)
    .range(d3.scale.category10().range());
```

Now we can start rendering the visuals, starting with the axes:

```
var yAxis = d3.svg.axis().scale(yScale).orient('left');
var yAxisNodes = svg.append('g')
    .attr('transform', 'translate(' +
        (margin.left - axisPadding) + ',' + margin.top + ')')
    .call(yAxis);
styleAxisNodes(yAxisNodes);
```

```
var xAxis = d3.svg.axis().scale(xScale).orient('bottom');
var xAxisNodes = svg.append('g')
    .attr('transform', 'translate(' + margin.left + ',' +
        (totalHeight - margin.bottom + axisPadding) + ')')
    .call(xAxis);
styleAxisNodes(xAxisNodes);
```

The final task is to render the bubbles:

```
svg.append('g')
    .attr('transform', 'translate(' + margin.left + ',' +
                                    margin.top + ')')
    .selectAll('circle')
    .data(data)
    .enter()
    .append('circle')
    .each(function(d) {
        d3.select(this).attr({
            cx: xScale(d.LifeExp),
            cy: yScale(d.FertRate),
            r: popScale(d.Population),
            fill: regionColorMap(d.Region),
            stroke: regionColorMap(d.Region),
            'fill-opacity': 0.5
        });
    });
```

Summary

In this chapter, we put together several examples of creating scatter and bubble plots. You learned a number of techniques for organizing data that represents between two and four distinct dimensions, using axes for two of the dimensions, and then using color and size-of-points as two more.

In the next chapter, we will begin with animation. We will start with the fundamentals of animation, and by the end of the chapter, we will extend this chapter's final example and use animation to represent an extra dimension, a fifth dimension — time.

7
Creating Animated Visuals

We are now going to look at using D3.js transitions to represent changes in the information underlying a visual. We will start with examples for examining several concepts involved in using D3.js to animate the properties of visual elements from one state to another.

By the end of this chapter, we will extend the bubble visualization from *Chapter 6, Creating Scatter and Bubble Plots*, to demonstrate how we can animate our bubbles as we move through multiple years of data. This will demonstrate the construction of a relatively complex animation through which a user can easily deduce trends in the information.

In this chapter, we will cover the following topics through examples:

- Animating using transitions
- Animating the fill color of a rectangle
- Animating multiple properties simultaneously
- Delaying an animation
- Creating chained transitions
- Handling the start and end events of transitions
- Changing the content and size of text using tweening
- Using timers to schedule the steps of an animation
- Adding a fifth dimension to a bubble chart through animation: time

Introduction to animation

D3.js provides extensive capabilities for animating your visualizations. Through the use of animation, we can provide the viewer with a means to understanding how data changes over time.

Animation in D3.js is all about changing the properties of the visual objects over time. When these properties are changed, the DOM is updated and the visual is modified to represent the new state.

To animate properties, D3.js provides the following capabilities that we will examine:

- Transitions
- Interpolators and tweenings
- Easings
- Timers

Animating using transitions

D3.js animations are implemented via the concept of **transitions**. Transitions provide instructions and information to D3.js for changing one or more visual attribute values over a specific duration of time.

When D3.js starts a transition on a visual, it calculates the initial style and ending style for the element that is being transitioned. These are often referred to as the start and end **keyframes**. Each keyframe is a set of styles and other properties that you can specify as part of the animation. D3.js will then animate those properties from the start values to the end values.

Animating the fill color of a rectangle

To demonstrate a transition in action, we will start with an example and animate the color of a rectangle from one color to another. The code for this example is available at the following link:

[bl.ock (7.1): http://goo.gl/oNJOQ9   ]

In this example, we start by creating the following SVG rectangle and setting its initial `fill` to `red`, followed by transitioning the fill color to `blue` over a period of five seconds.

When running the example, you will see a single rectangle that changes from red to blue over a period of five seconds. During that time, it smoothly animates through intermediate colors such as purple, as seen in the following image:

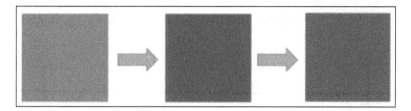

The primary part of this code that does the animation is the following; it starts by creating the rectangle and setting its initial color to red:

```
svg.append('rect')
    .attr({
        x: '10px',
        y: '10px',
        width: 80,
        height: 80,
        fill: 'red'
    })
    .transition()
    .duration(5000)
    .attr({ fill: 'blue' });
```

The call to `.transition()` informs D3.js that we we want to transition one or more properties of the rect element that are made to the attributes of the rect element using calls to .style() or .attr().

The call to `.transition()` instructs D3.js to track any changes that are made to the attributes of the SVG element using calls to `.style()` or `.attr()`.

In this case, we specify that the `fill` of the rectangle should be `blue` at the end of the transition. D3.js uses this to calculate the starting and ending keyframes, which tracks the fill on the rectangle should change from red to blue in this case.

When the rendering of these elements begins, D3.js also starts the animation and smoothly changes the fill property over the specified period.

Animating multiple properties simultaneously

Multiple properties can be animated on an object during a transition. To accomplish this, all that is required is to set multiple attributes after the call to `.transition()`.

As an example, the following code animates the position of the rectangle and its size over the five-second period:

bl.ock (7.2): `http://goo.gl/2qG0EV`

The code extends the previous example by animating not only the fill, but also by changing the position to move the rectangle along a diagonal, and modifying the size to make the rectangle half the width and height at the end of the transition:

```
svg.append('rect')
    .attr({
        x: 10,
        y: 10,
        width: 80,
        height: 80,
        fill: 'red'
    })
    .transition()
    .duration(5000)
    .attr({
        x: 460,
        y: 150,
        width: 40,
        height: 40,
        fill: 'blue'
    });
```

The resulting animation looks like the following image, where the rectangle moves along the path of the arrows, while changing both, color and size:

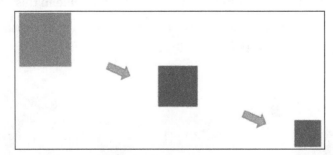

Delaying a transition

If you do not want an animation to start instantaneously, you can use a delay. A delay defers the start of the transition for the specified period of time.

The following example defers the start of the transition for one second, then runs the transition for four seconds, completing the transition in an overall time of five seconds.

bl.ock (7.3): `http://goo.gl/Vyd6Pd`

The code for the preceding example is the same as the previous one except for the following lines:

```
.transition()
.delay(1000)
.duration(4000)
```

Creating chained transitions

A single transition changes the properties between only one set of keyframes. However, it is possible to chain transitions together for providing multiple sequences of animations. The following example demonstrates the chaining of two transitions (and also a delay at the start).

bl.ock (7.4): `http://goo.gl/IfYJmY`

The first transition is executed for two seconds and animates the size, color, and position of the rectangle to the middle of the SVG area. The second transition then moves the rectangle to the upper-right corner for another two seconds while still continuing to change its color and size. The total execution time remains five seconds:

```
svg.append('rect')
    .attr({
        x: 10,
        'y': 10,
        width: 80,
        height: 80,
        fill: 'red'
    })
```

```
.transition()
.delay(1000)
.duration(2000)
.attr({
    x: 240,
    y: 80,
    width: 60,
    height: 60,
    fill: 'purple'
})
.transition()
.duration(2000)
.attr({
    width: 40,
    height: 40,
    x: 460,
    y: 10,
    fill: 'blue'
});
```

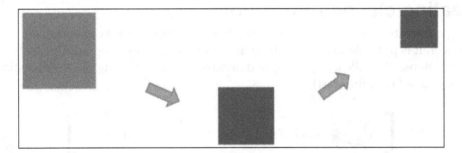

Handling the start and end events of transitions

It is possible to handle the start and end events of a transition using the .each() function. This is useful for ensuring that the starting or ending style is exactly what you desire at the start or end of the transition. This can be an issue when interpolators (covered in the next section) are at and exact expected value, where the start values are not known until the animation is running, or there are browser-specific issues that need to be addressed.

An example of a browser issue is that of transparent colors being represented by rgba(0,0,0,0). This is black but completely transparent. However, an animation using this will always start with fully opaque black. The start event can be used to patch up the color at the start of the animation.

The following example demonstrates hooking on to the start event of the first transition and the end event of the second transition by modifying the previous example:

bl.ock (7.5): `http://goo.gl/746hLo`

There are two fundamental changes in this example. The hooking on to the start event of the first transition changes the color of the rectangle to green. This causes the rectangle to flash from red to green just after the delay finishes:

```
.each('start', function() {
    d3.select(this).attr({ fill: 'green' });
})
```

The following code shows the second change, which reforms the rectangle to yellow at the end of the second animation:

```
.each('end', function() {
    d3.select(this).attr({ fill: 'yellow' });
});
```

Note that when using the `.each()` function, the function that is called loses the context of the selection, and does not know the current item. We can get that back using the call to `d3.select(this)`, which will return the current datum that the functions are being applied to.

In my experience, I have found that the setting of attributes before and after transitions must use a consistent notation. If you use `.style()` prior to the transition, and then `.attr()` later, even on the same attribute, the transition will not work for that attribute. So, if you use `.style()` before `.transition()`, make sure to use `.style()` after (and vice versa for `.attr()`).

Changing the content and size of text using tweening

Tweening provides a means of telling D3.js the way to calculate property values during transitions without D3.js tracking the keyframes. Keyframes can be a performance issue when animating a large quantity of items, so tweening can help out in such situations.

Tweening gives us the opportunity to connect in our own **interpolator** for providing values at each step during an animation. An interpolator is a function that is passed a single value between 0.0 and 1.0, which represents the current percentage of the transition completed. The implementation of the interpolator then uses this value to calculate the value at that point in time.

We will look at two examples of tweening. The first example, available at the following link, animates the value of a text item from 0 to 10 over a period of ten seconds:

bl.ock (7.6): `http://goo.gl/SlWBdp`

This is actually something that cannot be done using attribute animation. We must call the `.text()` function of the DOM element to set the text, so we cannot use that technique to animate the change in content. We have to use tweening. The following snippet from the example creates the tween that sets the text content during the animation:

```
svg.append('text')
    .attr({ x: 10, y: 50 })
    .transition()
    .duration(10000)
    .tween("mytween", function () {
        return function(t) {
            this.textContent = d3.interpolateRound(0, 10)(t);
        }
    });
```

The first parameter to `.tween()` is simply a name for this tween. The second parameter is a factory function which returns another function to D3.js that will be called at each step during the transition, passing it the current percentage of transition completed.

The factory function is called once for each datum at the start of the animation. The function it returns is called repeatedly, and uses the `d3.interpolateRound()` function to return rounded numbers between 0 and 10 based upon the value of `t`.

There are a number of interpolation functions provided by D3.js, such as:

- `d3.interpolateNumber`
- `d3.interpolateRound`
- `d3.interpolateString`
- `d3.interpolateRgb`
- `d3.interpolateHsl`
- `d3.interpolateLab`
- `d3.interpolateHcl`
- `d3.interpolateArray`
- `d3.interpolateObject`
- `d3.interpolateTransform`
- `d3.interpolateZoom`

D3.js also has a function `d3.interpolate(a, b)`, which returns the appropriate interpolation function from the previous list based upon the type of the end value b, using the following algorithm:

- If b is a color, `interpolateRgb` is used
- If b is a string, `interpolateString` is used
- If b is an array, `interpolateArray` is used
- If b is an object and not coercible to a number, `interpolateObject` is used
- Otherwise, `interpolateNumber` is used

For a demonstration of `d3.interpolate()` and some of the underlying smarts, open the following example:

bl.ock (7.7): `http://goo.gl/7921pH`

This example uses the `.styleTween()` function to change the font property of the style for the piece of text, increasing the size of the font from 12 px to 36 px over five seconds.

```
svg.append("text")
    .attr({ x: 10, y: 50 })
    .text('Watch my size change')
    .transition()
    .duration(5000)
    .styleTween('font', function() {
        return d3.interpolate('12px Helvetica', '36px Helvetica');
    });
```

The `.styleTween()` function operates in a way similar to `.tween()` except that the first parameter specifies the name of the property that will be set to the value which is returned by the interpolation function provided by the factory method. There is also a `.attrTween()` function that does the same but on an attribute instead of a style.

The function `d3.interpolate()` is smart enough to determine that it should use `d3.interpolateString()`, and to identify that the two strings represent a font size and name besides performing the appropriate interpolation.

Timers

D3.js manages transitions using timers that internally schedule the code to be run at a specific time. These timers are also exposed for your use.

A timer can be created using `d3.timer(yourFunction, [delay], [mark])`, which takes a function to be called, a delay, and a starting time. This starting time is referred to as the **mark**, and it has a default value of `Date.now`.

D3.js timers are not executed at regular intervals—they are not periodic timers. Timers start execution at the time specified by mark + delay. The function will then be called as frequently as possible by D3.js, until the function it calls returns true.

The use of mark and delay can allow very specific declaration of time for starting execution. As an example, the following command schedules an event four hours prior to September 1, 2015:

```
d3.timer(notify, -4 * 1000 * 60 * 60, +new Date(2015, 09, 01));
```

To implement a one-shot timer, simply return true from the first call of the function.

As a final note on timers, if you want to use a timer to alert you on a regular basis, it is often better to use the JavaScript built-in function setInterval(). We will examine using a timer on a periodic basis in the following section.

Adding a fifth dimension to a bubble plot – time

Now let's apply everything we have learned about animation to some real data. We are going to revisit our bubble plot visualization from *Chapter 6, Creating Scatter and Bubble Plots,* expanding the set of data from a single year (2013) to all the available years (1960 through 2013). We will modify the rendering of the visual to periodically update and animate the bubbles into new position and sizes based upon the change in the values of the data.

The expanded data set is available at https://goo.gl/rC5WS0. The fundamental difference is the inclusion of a year column, and data covering 54 years.

The code for and the demo of the example is available at the following link:

bl.ock (7.7): http://goo.gl/iYCNbG

When you run this, you will see a smooth animation of the data over the years. It is obviously impossible to show this effectively in a static medium such as a book. But for demonstration, I have provided screenshots of the visualization at the start of each decade, except for 2010, which is substituted with the year 2013:

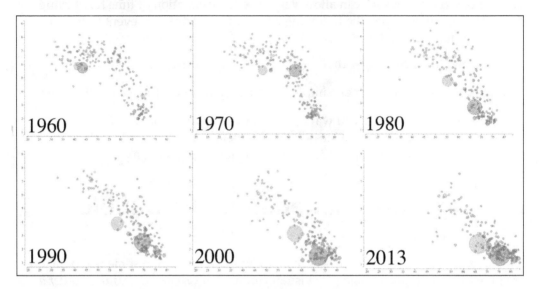

As the years advance, there is a strong tendency for all the countries towards an increased lifespan as well as decrease in fertility. This happens at a different pace for different countries. But it gives you a really good sense that something is going on that is causing this effect. Deciphering the plot is further made easier due to the addition of this extra dimension of time to the bubble plot.

Now let's examine how this is implemented in the example. A good portion of the code is identical to that of the example from *Chapter 6, Creating Scatter and Bubble Plots*, which it is based upon. The loading and cleansing of the data is slightly different due to a different URL and the need to process the Year column in the data:

```
var url = "https://gist.githubusercontent.com/
d3byex/8fcf43e446b1e4dd0146/raw/7a11679cb4a810061dee660be0d30b6a9fe6
9f26/lfp_all.csv";
d3.csv(url, function (error, rawData) {
    var data = rawData.map(function (d) {
        return {
            CountryCode: d.CountryCode,
            CountryName: d.CountryName,
```

```
        LifeExp: +d.LifeExp,
        FertRate: +d.FertRate,
        Population: +d.Population,
        Region: d.Region,
        Year: d.Year
    };
});
```

We will be rendering each year of data one at a time. As a part of this, we will need to extract only the data for each specific year. There are a number of ways that we can go about this. D3.js provides a very powerful function to do this for us: d3.nest(). This function pivots the Year column into the index of an associative array:

```
var nested = d3.nest()
    .key(function (d) { return d.Year; })
    .sortKeys(d3.ascending)
    .map(data);
```

We can then access all the data for a particular year using array semantics such as nested[1975], which will give us the data (only the rows) for just 1975.

For more info on d3.nest(), see https://github.com/mbostock/d3/wiki/Arrays#-nest.

The code is then identical through the creation of the axes. The next new piece of code is to add a text label on the graph to show the year that the data represents. This is positioned in the lower-left corner of the area where the bubbles will be rendered:

```
var yearLabel = svg.append('g')
    .append('text')
    .attr('transform', 'translate(40, 450)')
    .attr('font-size', '75');
```

Then a group is created to contain the bubbles. The rendering function will select this group each time it is called:

```
var bubblesHolder = svg.append('g');
```

This marks the beginning of the code that renders and animates the bubbles. It starts by declaring the interval for which each year should be drawn (10 times per second):

```
var interval = 100;
```

Since the bubbles must be repeatedly rendered, we create a function that can be called to render the bubbles for just a specified year:

```
function render(year) {
    var dataForYear = nested[year];

    var bubbles = bubblesHolder
        .selectAll("circle")
        .data(dataForYear, function (datum) {
            return datum.CountryCode;
        });

    bubbles.enter()
        .append("circle")
        .each(setItemAttributes);

    bubbles
        .transition()
        .duration(interval)
        .each(setItemAttributes);

    bubbles.exit().remove();

    yearLabel.text(year);
};
```

This function first extracts the rows for the specific year, and then binds the data to the circles in the `bubblesHolder` group. The call to `.data()` also specifies that `CountryCode` will be used as the key. This is very important, because as we move from year to year, D3.js will use this to map the existing bubbles to the new data, making decisions based on this the key on which to enter-update-exit the circles.

The next statement executes the enter function creating new circles and calling a function to set the various attributes of the circles:

```
function setItemAttributes(d) {
    d3.select(this).attr({
        cx: xScale(d.LifeExp),
        cy: yScale(d.FertRate),
        r: popScale(d.Population),
        style: "fill:" + regionColorMap(d.Region) + ";" +
            "fill-opacity:0.5;" +
            "stroke:" + regionColorMap(d.Region) + ";"
    });
};
```

We use a function, as this is also used by the code to update. Finally, there is a case where occasionally a country disappears from the data, so we will remove any bubbles in the scenario.

The final thing we need to do is perform the time animation. This is done by iterating through each year at the specified interval. To do this, we need to know the start and ending year, which we can obtain with the following:

```
var minYear = d3.min(data, function (d) { return d.Year; });
var maxYear = d3.max(data, function (d) { return d.Year; });
```

This follows with setting a variable for the current year and rendering that year:

```
var currentYear = minYear;
render(currentYear);
```

Now we create a function to be called by a timer. This function returns another function which increments the year, and if the year is less than the max year, calls render again, and then schedules another timer instance to run at an interval of milliseconds. This pattern effectively uses a series of D3.js timers for implementing the periodic timer:

```
var callback = function () {
    return function () {
        currentYear++;
        console.log(currentYear);
        if (currentYear <= maxYear) {
            render(currentYear);
            d3.timer(callback(), interval);
        }
        return true;
    }
}
```

 Note that this code returns `true` every time it is called. This makes it a one-shot timer. But before returning `true`, if we need to render another year, we start another timer.

The last thing to be done is to start the timer for the first time:

```
d3.timer(callback(), interval);
```

Summary

In this chapter, you learned the fundamentals of animation in D3.js, and by the end of the chapter, applied these simple concepts to make what appears to be a very complex data visualization.

We started with examples of transitions, using them to animate attributes from one state to another across an interval of time, and chaining animations together. Next we looked at handling animation without keyframes using tweening. We also took a quick look at interpolation.

We finished by examining timers, and then applied all the concepts of the chapter to progressively render a large set of data, giving the viewer of the visualization a sense of how data changes by animating time.

In the next chapter, we will examine changing the visuals when the user interacts with the application, learning concepts such as the dragging and filtering of data based upon interactive events.

8

Adding User Interactivity

Great visualizations provide more than a pretty picture and animations; they allow the user to interact with the data, giving them the ability to play with the data to discover the meaning in the data that may not be obvious through a given static presentation.

Exceptional interactions allow the users to steer their way through large amounts of information. It allows them to pan through data too large for a single display, to dive into summary information, and also zoom out to get a higher level view—in essence, it allows users to see the forest from the trees.

Also of great value is the capability to allow the user to easily select, reorder, and reposition visual elements. Through these actions, the user is able to see details of a datum simply by mouseover or touch, to rearrange items for exposing other insights, and to also see how data moves around when reordered. This provides the user a sense of constancy and shows how the data changes when asked to reshuffle on demand.

In this chapter, we will examine a number of techniques for adding interactivity to your D3.js visualizations. We will examine concepts involved in using the mouse to highlight information and provide contextual information, to pan and zoom your visualizations, and to use brushing to select and zoom the view of information in and out.

Specifically, in this chapter we will learn the following topics:

- Hooking into mouse events on D3.js visuals
- Clicking and responding to mouse events
- Building several models of visual animation to provide feedback on interaction
- Handling mouse hovers to provide detailed information on specific visuals
- Creating fluid animations that respond to mouse events
- Brushing and its use in selecting data
- Implementing a context-focus pattern of interaction for viewing stock data

Handling mouse events

The mouse is the most common device available to users for interacting with D3.js visualizations. Touch is commonly used in case of tablets, and in many cases, touch events can be mapped to mouse events. In this chapter, we will focus exclusively on the mouse. But most of everything we cover also applies to touch. Touch concepts such as pinching can also be easily supported on touch devices with D3.js.

To work with mouse events in D3.js, we attach event listeners to the SVG elements for which we desire to handle the events. The handlers are added using the `.on()` function, which takes as parameters the name of the event and a function to call when the mouse event happens.

We will examine the handling of four mouse events: `mousemove`, `mouseenter`, `mouseout`, and `click`.

Tracking the mouse position using mousemove

The movement of the mouse on an SVG visual is reported to your code by listening for the `mousemove` event. This following example demonstrates tracking and reporting the mouse position:

bl.ock (8.1): `http://goo.gl/VK67C4`

```
var svg = d3.select('body')
    .append('svg')
    .attr({
        width: 450,
        height: 450
    });
var label = svg.append('text')
    .attr('x', 10)
    .attr('y', 30);

svg.on('mousemove', function () {
    var position = d3.mouse(svg.node());
    label.text('X=' + position[0] + ' , Y=' + position[1]);
});
```

We listen to mousemove events using .on(), passing it when the event fires, and the example updates the content of the text in the SVG text element:

X=100 , Y=44

The position of the mouse is not passed to the function as parameters. To get the actual mouse position, we need to call the d3.mouse() function, passing it to the return value of svg.node(). This function then calculates the X and Y mouse position relative to the SVG element for which the mouse is moving over.

Capturing the mouse entering and exiting an SVG element

The mouse entering and exiting a particular SVG element is captured using the respective mouseenter and mouseout events. The following example shows this by creating several circles and then changing their color while the mouse is within the area of the circle (also known as **hovering**).

bl.ock (8.2): http://goo.gl/4cfrdq

This code creates three circles of varying size (30, 20, and 40 pixel radius):

```
var data = [30, 20, 40],
```

Tracking the enter and exit of the mouse is performed by hooking into those two events:

```
.on('mouseenter', function() {
    d3.select(this).attr('fill', 'red');
})
.on('mouseout', function() {
    d3.select(this).attr('fill', 'steelblue');
});
```

When you run this example, you will be presented by three `steelblue` circles of slightly varying size, and when you hover the mouse over any of them you will see it change to `red`:

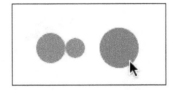

Note that the SVG element which the mouse is currently entering or exiting is not passed to the functions, so we need to retrieve them using `d3.select(this)`.

Letting the user know they have clicked the mouse

When the user clicks a button on the mouse, the mouse can track the mouse being clicked by using the `mouseclick` event. The code at the following link demonstrates handling the click event handler:

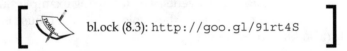

bl.ock (8.3): `http://goo.gl/91rt4S`

This code adds an event handler to the code in example *8.2* to capture the click event and pop up an alert box that shows the value of the datum and its position in the collection:

```
.on('click', function(d, i) {
    alert(d + ' ' + i);
});
```

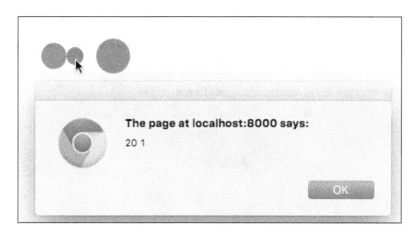

This is pretty neat as you are given the data underlying the visual that you clicked. There is no need to retain a map of the visuals to the data to just look this up.

Using behaviors to drag, pan, and zoom

Mouse events often need to be combined to create more complex interactions such as drag, pan, and zoom. Normally, this requires a good quantity of code to track sequences of the mouseenter, mousemove, and mouseexit events.

D3.js provides us with a better way of implementing these interactions through the use of **behaviors**. These behaviors are a complex set of DOM/SVG interactions through D3.js itself handling the mouse events. In a sense, behaviors function similarly to gesture recognizers on mobile platforms.

D3.js currently provides two built-in behaviors:

- **Drag**: This tracks mouse or multi-touch movements relative to an origin
- **Zoom**: This emits zoom and pan events in response to dragging or pinching

Let's examine an example of implementing drag and another that also adds pan and zoom capabilities.

Drag

Drag is a common behavior in interactive visualization that allows the movement of visual elements by the user via the mouse or touch. The following example demonstrates using the drag behavior:

bl.ock (8.4): `http://goo.gl/wxn6iN`

The preceding example renders four circles and lets you move them around the SVG area using the mouse, but also constrains the movement so that the circles remain completely within the SVG element's visual area:

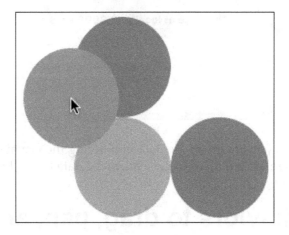

The code begins by calculating the positions for the circles and rendering them using a selection. The drag behavior is then implemented with the following code:

```
var dragBehavior = d3.behavior.drag()
                            .on('drag', onDrag);
circles.call(dragBehavior);

function onDrag(d) {
    var x = d3.event.x,
        y = d3.event.y;
    if ((x >= radius) && (x <= width - radius) &&
        (y >= radius) && (y <= height - radius)) {
        d3.select(this)
```

```
        .attr('transform', function () {
            return 'translate(' + x + ', ' + y + ')';
        });
    }
}
```

The behavior is created using d3.behavior.drag(). This object then requires us to tell it that we are interested in listening to drag events. You can also specify handlers for dragstart and dragged events to identify the start and completion of a drag behavior.

Next, we need to inform D3.js to hook up the behavior to SVG elements. This is done by using the .call() function on the selection. As we saw when rendering axes, the function we specified will be called by D3.js during the rendering of each selected item. In this case, this will be our drag behavior, and hence, the implementation of this function can perform all the event processing needed for dragging an SVG element on our behalf.

Our event handler for the drag behavior is then called whenever the user drags an associated SVG element. This function first retrieves the new x and y position for the item being dragged from the d3.event object. These values are computed and set by D3.js prior to this function being called.

All that is required at this point is to set a new transform for the respective SVG element to move it into the new position. This example also checks that the circle is still completely within the SVG element and only sets the new position if that is true.

Pan and zoom

Panning and zooming are two common techniques in data visualization. Panning allows the user to drag the entire visual around the screen. This exposes visuals that would otherwise be rendered outside of the bounds of the visual area. A common scenario for panning is to move a map around to expose areas previously out of view.

Zooming allows you to scale up or down the perceived distance of the user from the visual. This can be used to make small items bigger or to zoom out to see items that were too big or out of the extent of the visual display.

Both panning and zooming are implemented by the same D3.js behavior, d3.behavior.zoom(). The following example demonstrates its use:

bl.ock (8.5): http://goo.gl/tEY0hm

When running this example, you can not only drag the circles, but you can drag the background to move all the circles at once (the pan) and use your mouse wheel to zoom in and out:

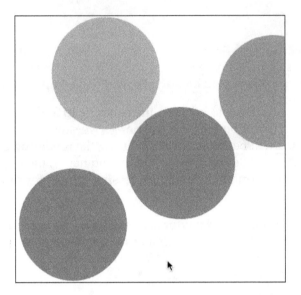

There are a few small changes to the previous example for adding these additional features. These start with the declaration of the zoom behavior:

```
var zoomBehavior = d3.behavior.zoom()
    .scaleExtent([0.1, 10])
    .on('zoom', onZoom);
```

The initial zoom level is 1.0. The call to .scaleExtent() informs the behavior that it should zoom down to 0.1, one-tenth of the original size, and up to 10, or 10x of the original. Moreover, the behavior should call the onZoom() function when zoom events occur .

Now we create the main SVG element and attach the zoom behavior to it using .call():

```
var svg = d3.select('body')
    .append('svg')
    .attr({
        width: width,
        height: height
    })
    .call(zoomBehavior)
    .append('g');
```

The code also appends a group element to the SVG element and the svg variable then refers to this group. The pan and zoom events are routed by the top level SVG element to our handler, which then sets the translate and scale factor on this group, therefore creating the effects on the circles.

Now we just need to implement the zoomIt function:

```
function onZoom() {
    svg.attr('transform', 'translate(' + d3.event.translate +
            ')' + 'scale(' + d3.event.scale + ')');
}
```

Just before the behavior calls this function, it sets the d3.event.translate variable to represent the extent of translation that should occur on the entire visual.

The d3.event.scale variable is also set by D3.js to represent the appropriate level of zoom. In this example, this ranges from 0.1 to 10.

Another small change is in the way the drag behavior is declared.

```
var dragBehavior = d3.behavior.drag()
    .on("drag", onDrag)
    .on("dragstart", function() {
        d3.event.sourceEvent.stopPropagation();
    });
```

This is done because there will be an issue with the example if this is not modified in the preceding manner. If left as-is, the pan and zoom behavior and the drag behavior will conflict with each other. When dragging a circle, the svg element will also pan when it should stay in place.

By handling the dragstart event and calling d3.event.sourceEvent. stopPropagation(), we prevent this mouse event on a circle from bubbling up to the svg element and starting a pan. Problem solved!

Enhancing a bar graph with interactivity

Now let's apply what we have learned about mouse event handling to create an interactive bar graph. Mouse events on a bar chart can provide useful contextual information to the person interacting with the graph.

The data for the examples will use a stripped-down version of the life expectancy vs fertility dataset that was used in earlier chapters. This dataset will use the data for the Latin American and Caribbean economic regions only, which contain roughly 35 countries, for the year 2013.

The bars in the examples will represent the longevity, will be annotated at the top with the country code, and have vertically oriented text representing the actual longevity value and the full country name. The examples will omit axes and margins to keep things simple.

The code and live example for this example is available at the following location:

bl.ock (8.6): http://goo.gl/8jb9Rn

This interaction pattern can be used to visually accentuate a particular bar in a bar chart when the mouse is moved over it. We have seen this when using `mouseenter` and `mouseout` events earlier as applied to circles. Here, we will use it to highlight the bar:

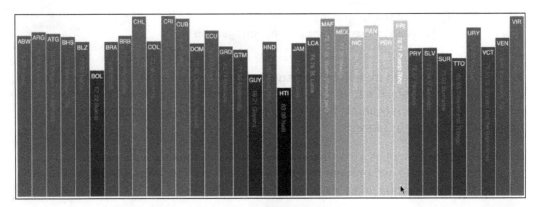

The rectangles representing the bars are created with the following code:

```
svg.selectAll('rect')
    .data(data)
    .enter()
    .append('rect')
    .attr({
        width: barWidth,
        height: 0,
        y: height
    })
```

After the creation of the bars, the code hooks up the `mouseover` and `mouseout` events. The `mouseover` event makes the vertical text completely opaque and sets the bar color to orange:

```
.on('mouseover', function (d) {
    d3.select('text.vert#' + d.CountryCode)
      .style('opacity', maxOpacity);
    d3.select(this).attr('fill', 'orange');
})
```

The `mouseout` event animates and sets the text opacity back to the original value and starts an animation to set the color back to its original shade. This animation gives the appearance of mouse trails when moving across the bars:

```
.on('mouseout', function (d) {
    d3.select('text.vert#' + d.CountryCode)
      .style('opacity', minOpacity);
    d3.select(this)
      .transition()
      .duration(returnToColorDuration)
      .attr('fill', 'rgb(0, 0, ' +
                    Math.floor(colorScale(d.LifeExp)) + ')');
})
```

The last portion of the selection creating the bars performs an animation to make the bars grow and transition from black to their eventual colors which the graph loads:

```
.transition()
.duration(barGrowDuration)
.attr({
    height: function (d) { return yScale(d.LifeExp); },
    x: function (d, i) { return xScale(i); },
    y: function (d) {
        return height - yScale(d.LifeExp);
    },
    fill: function (d) {
        return 'rgb(0, 0, ' +
                Math.floor(colorScale(d.LifeExp)) + ')';
    }
});
```

To also enhance the presentation of the underlying information, we will place two pieces of data on each bar: the country code as horizontal text at the top and a piece of vertical text which shows the actual value of the datum and the full name of the country. The following code creates the horizontal text:

```
svg.selectAll('text')
    .data(data)
    .enter()
    .append('text')
    .text(function (d) { return d.CountryCode; })
    .attr({
        x: function (d, i) { return xScale(i) + barWidth / 2; },
        y: height,
        fill: 'white',
        'text-anchor': 'middle',
        'font-family': 'sans-serif',
        'font-size': '11px'
    })
    .transition()
    .duration(barGrowDuration)
    .attr('y', function (d) {
                    return height - yScale(d.LifeExp) +
                                        horzTextOffsetY; });
```

The vertical text is created by the following code:

```
svg.selectAll('text.vert')
    .data(data)
    .enter()
    .append('text')
    .text(function (d) { return d.LifeExp.toFixed(2) + ' ' +
                                d.CountryName; })
    .attr({
        id: function (d) { return d.CountryCode; },
        opacity: minOpacity,
        transform: function (d, i) {
            var x = xScale(i) + halfBarWidth -
                    verticalTextOffsetX;
            var y = height - yScale(d.LifeExp) +
                    verticalTextOffsetY;
            return 'translate(' + x + ',' + y + ')rotate(90)';
        },
        'class': 'vert',
```

```
            'font-family': 'sans-serif',
            'font-size': 11,
            'fill': 'white'
    });
```

Highlighting selected items using brushes

A **brush** in D3.js provides the ability for the user to interact with your visualization by allowing the selection of one or more visual elements (and the underlying data items) using the mouse.

This is a very important concept in exploratory data analysis and visualization, as it allows users to easily drill in and out of data or select specific data items for further analysis.

Brushing in D3.js is very flexible, and how you implement it depends upon the type of visualization you are presenting to the user. We will look at several examples or brushes and then implement a real example that lets us use a brush to examine stock data.

Online examples of brushes

To understand brushes, let's first take a look at several brush examples on the Internet. These are all examples available on the web that you can go and play with.

The following brush shows the use of rectangular selection for selecting data that is within the brush (http://bl.ocks.org/mbostock/4343214):

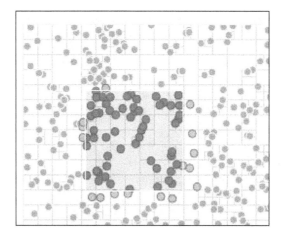

Another example of this brushing is the scatterplot matrix brush at `http://bl.ocks.org/mbostock/4063663`. This example is notable for the way in which you can select points on any one of the scatter plots. The app then selects the points on all the other plots so that the data is highlighted on those too:

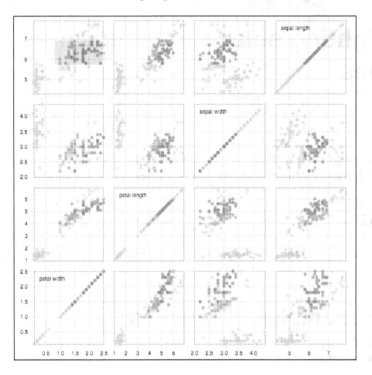

The following example demonstrates using a brush to select a point within a force-directed network visualization (`http://bl.ocks.org/mbostock/4565798`):

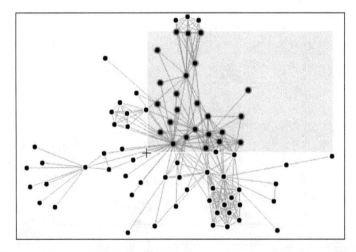

We will learn about force-directed network visualizations in greater detail in *Chapter 11, Visualizing Information Networks*.

The creation of custom brush handles is a common scenario you will see when using brushes. Handles provide you a means of providing a custom rendering of the edges of the brush to provide a visual cue to the user.

As an example of a custom brush, the following creates semicircles as the handles: `http://bl.ocks.org/mbostock/4349545`.

You can resize the brush by dragging either handle and reposition it by dragging the area between the handles:

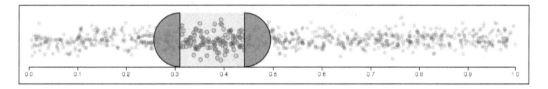

The last example of a brush (before we create our own) is the following, which demonstrates a concept referred to as `focus + context`:

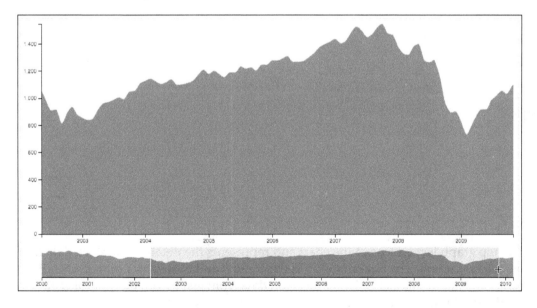

In this example, the brush is drawn atop the smaller graph (the context). The context graph is static in nature, showing a summary of the entire range of data. As the brush is changed upon the context, the larger graph (the focus) animates in real-time while the brush is changed.

In the next section, we will examine creating a similar version of this graph which utilizes financial data, a common domain for this type of interactive visualization.

Implementing focus + context

Now let's examine how to implement **focus + context**. The following example that we will use will apply this concept to a series of stock data:

bl.ock (8.7): http://goo.gl/Niyc56

The resulting graph will look like the following graph:

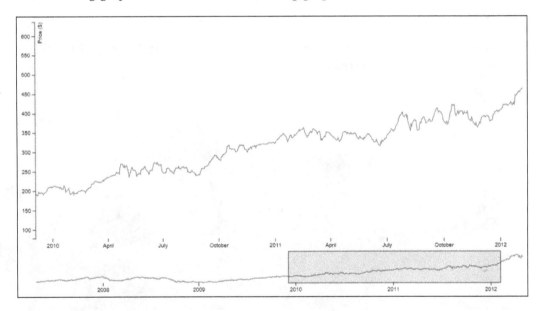

The top graph is the focus of the chart and represents the detail of the stock data that we are examining. The bottom graph is the context and is always a plot of the full series of data. In this example, we focus on data from just before the start of 2010 until just after the start of 2012.

The context area supports brushing. You can create a new brush by clicking on the context graph and dragging the mouse to select the extents of the brush. The brush can then be slid back and forth by dragging it, and it can be resized on the left and right by dragging either boundary. The focus area will always display the details of the area selected by the context.

To create this visualization, we will be drawing two different graphs, and hence, we need to layout the vertical areas for each and create the main SVG element with a size enough to hold both:

```
var width = 960, height = 600;

var margins = { top: 10, left: 50, right: 50,
                bottom: 50, between: 50 };

var bottomGraphHeight = 50;
var topGraphHeight = height - (margins.top + margins.bottom +
                               margins.between + bottomGraphHeight);
var graphWidths = width - margins.left - margins.right;
```

This example will also require the creation of a clipping area. As the line drawn in the focus area scales, it may be drawn overlapping on the left with the *y* axis. The clipping area prevents the line from flowing off to the left over the axis:

```
svg.append('defs')
    .append('clipPath')
    .attr('id', 'clip')
    .append('rect')
    .attr('width', width)
    .attr('height', height);
```

This clipping rectangle is referred to in the styling for the lines. When the lines are drawn, they will be clipped to this boundary. We will see how this is specified when examining the function to style the lines.

Now we add two groups that will hold the renderings for both the focus and context graphs:

```
var focus = svg
    .append('g')
    .attr('transform', 'translate(' + margins.left + ',' +
                               margins.top + ')');
```

```
var context = svg.append('g')
    .attr('class', 'context')
    .attr('transform', 'translate(' + margins.left + ',' +
            (margins.top + topGraphHeight + margins.between) + ')');
```

This visual requires one *y* axis, two *x* axes, and the appropriate scales for each. These are created with the following code:

```
var xScaleTop = d3.time.scale().range([0, graphWidths]),
    xScaleBottom = d3.time.scale().range([0, graphWidths]),
    yScaleTop = d3.scale.linear().range([topGraphHeight, 0]),
    yScaleBottom = d3.scale.linear()
                        .range([bottomGraphHeight, 0]);

var xAxisTop = d3.svg.axis().scale(xScaleTop)
                    .orient('bottom'),
    xAxisBottom = d3.svg.axis().scale(xScaleBottom)
                        .orient('bottom');
var yAxisTop = d3.svg.axis().scale(yScaleTop)
                        .orient('left');
```

We will be drawing two lines, so we create the two line generators, one for each of the lines:

```
var lineTop = d3.svg.line()
    .x(function (d) { return xScaleTop(d.date); })
    .y(function (d) { return yScaleTop(d.close); });

var lineBottom = d3.svg.line()
    .x(function (d) { return xScaleBottom(d.date); })
    .y(function (d) { return yScaleBottom(d.close); });
```

The last thing we need to do before loading the data and actually rendering it is to create our brush using d3.svg.brush():

```
var brush = d3.svg.brush()
    .x(xScaleBottom)
    .on('brush', function brushed() {
        xScaleTop.domain(brush.empty() ? xScaleBottom.domain() :
                                        brush.extent());
        focus.select('.x.axis').call(xAxisTop);
    });
```

This preceding snippet informs the brush that we want to brush along the x values using the scale defined in xScaleBottom. Brushes are event-driven and will handle the brush event, which is raised every time the brush is moved or resized.

And finally, the last major thing the code does is load the data and establish the initial visuals. You've seen this code before, so we won't explain it step by step. In short, it consists of loading the data, setting the domains on the scales, and adding and drawing the axes and lines:

```
d3.tsv('https://gist.githubusercontent.com/d3byex/
b6b753b6ef178fdb06a2/raw/0c13e82b6b59c3ba195d7f47c33e3fe00cc3f56f/
aapl.tsv', function (error, data) {
    data.forEach(function (d) {
        d.date = d3.time.format('%d-%b-%y').parse(d.date);
        d.close = +d.close;
    });

    xScaleTop.domain(d3.extent(data, function (d) {
                return d.date;
    }));
    yScaleTop.domain(d3.extent(data, function (d) {
        return d.close;
    }));
    xScaleBottom.domain(d3.extent(data, function (d) {
        return d.date;
    }));
    yScaleBottom.domain(d3.extent(data, function (d) {
        return d.close;
    }));

    var topXAxisNodes = focus.append('g')
        .attr('class', 'x axis')
        .attr('transform', 'translate(' + 0 + ',' +
                        (margins.top + topGraphHeight) + ')')
        .call(xAxisTop);
    styleAxisNodes(topXAxisNodes, 0);

    focus.append('path')
        .datum(data)
        .attr('class', 'line')
        .attr('d', lineTop);

    var topYAxisNodes = focus.append('g')
        .call(yAxisTop);
    styleAxisNodes(topYAxisNodes);

    context.append('path')
        .datum(data)
        .attr('class', 'line')
        .attr('d', lineBottom);
```

```
        var bottomXAxisNodes = context.append('g')
            .attr('transform', 'translate(0,' +
                                bottomGraphHeight + ')')
            .call(xAxisBottom);
        styleAxisNodes(bottomXAxisNodes, 0);

        context.append('g')
            .attr('class', 'x brush')
            .call(brush)
            .selectAll('rect')
            .attr('y', -6)
            .attr('height', bottomGraphHeight + 7);

        context.selectAll('.extent')
            .attr({
                stroke: '#000',
                'fill-opacity': 0.125,
                'shape-rendering': 'crispEdges'
            });

        styleLines(svg);
    });
```

Congratulations! You have stepped through creating a fairly complicated interactive display of stock data. But the beauty is that through the underlying capabilities of D3.js, it was comprised of a relatively small set of simple steps that result in **Beautiful Data**.

Summary

In this chapter, you learned how to use mouse events provided by D3.js to create interactive visualization. We started by explaining how to hook up mouse events and respond to them, changing the visualization as the events occurred. Then we examined behaviors and how we can use them to implement drag, pan, and zoom, which allow the user to move around data, take a closer look, as well as zoom in and out. Finally, we covered brushing and how it can be used to select multiple visuals/data items, ending with a slick example of applying **focus + context** to visualize financial data.

In the next chapter on layouts, we will move a little higher up the visual stack of D3.js to examine layouts, which are essentially generators for complex data visualizations.

9
Complex Shapes Using Paths

In *Chapter 3, Creating Visuals with SVG*, we briefly examined the concept of paths. We saw that we could use paths and their associated mini-language to create multi-segment renderings by creating a sequence of commands. These paths, although very powerful, can be cumbersome to create manually.

But don't fret, as D3.js provides a number of objects to create complex paths using just a few JavaScript statements. These **path generators** take much of the pain out of creating complex paths manually, as they do the heavy lifting of assembling the sequence of commands automatically.

Additionally, an important type of graph we have not looked at in this book is a line graph. This has been purposefully pushed off until now, as it is the most commonly used to create lines using path generators. After the examples in this chapter, the power of the path to create lines will be evident.

In this chapter, we will cover the following topics:

- An overview of path data generators
- Lines and area generators
- Arcs and pie generators
- Symbols generators
- Diagonals and radial generators
- Line interpolators

An overview of path data generators

D3.js goes to great lengths to make using SVG easy, particularly when creating complex paths. To do this, D3 provides a number of helper functions referred to as path generators that have been created to handle the gory details of path generation from a set of data.

The generators we examine will follow a common pattern of usage, so once you learn to use one, the use of the others will come naturally. These steps include:

1. Creating the `generator` object.
2. Specifying accessor functions that can be used to find the X and Y values.
3. Calling any additional methods to specify various rendering instructions.
4. Adding a path to the visual.
5. Specifying the data using `.datum()` on that path.
6. And finally, setting the d attribute of the path to the generator, which tells the path where to find the `generator` object for the path.

Once these are completed and D3.js renders the visual, it uses the generator that is attached to a d attribute and creates path commands based on your data. This is also why we use `.datum()` instead of `.data()`, as datum assigns the data to just that one element and does not force the execution of an enter-update-exit loop on that data.

Now let's examine doing this with various common generators—this will be fun!

Creating a sequence of lines

The line generator creates the necessary commands to draw a sequence of lines that are connected to each other:

bl.ock (9.1): `http://goo.gl/eAgBjL`

The preceding example creates a single line path generator and renders it twice, resulting in the following graphics:

The path generator is created with the following data and using a d3.svg.line() object. On that object, we call two functions, x() and y(), which we give a function that tells the generator how to locate the X and Y values for each datum:

```
var data = [
    { X: 10, Y: 10 },
    { X: 60, Y: 60 },
    { X: 80, Y: 20 }
];
var generator = d3.svg.line()
    .x(function(d) { return d.X; })
    .y(function(d) { return d.Y; });
```

The next step is to add a path, call its .datum() function passing the data, and setting the d attribute at a minimum to specify which generator to use. The example creates two paths that use the same data and generator but apply a different fill:

```
svg.append('path')
    .datum(data)
    .attr({
        d: generator,
        fill: 'none',
        stroke: 'steelblue'
    });
svg.append('path')
    .datum(data)
    .attr({
        transform: 'translate(100,0)',
        d: generator,
        fill: 'none',
        stroke: 'steelblue'
    });
```

This path specifies two lines. The default operation for a line path is to connect the last point with the first and fill in the internals. In the case of the first path, this is a black fill and results in the black triangle (if you zoom in, you will see the steelblue outline on two of the sides). The latter path sets the fill to empty, so the result is just the two lines.

This example also demonstrates using a single path generator but applying a transform and a different style to the actual path.

Examining the generated SVG, we see that D3.js has created the two paths and automatically generated the path data that is assigned to the d property of the path:

```
▼ <svg width="500" height="250">
    <path d="M10,10L60,60L80,20" stroke="steelblue"></path>
    <path transform="translate(100,0)" d="M10,10L60,60L80,20"
    fill="none" stroke="steelblue"></path>
  </svg>
```

Areas

An area path generator allows us to make line plots where the area below the line plot is filled in with a particular color. A practical use of these is for the creation of area graphs. The following example demonstrates the creation of an area graph:

bl.ock (9.2): `http://goo.gl/7Xmo7u`

This preceding example results in something that looks like the following image. The data is random, so it will be different each time it runs:

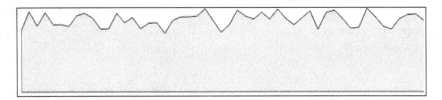

The data is generated by generating 100 random numbers between 0 and 30, and defining Y as the random value and X increasing in increments of 10:

```
var data = d3.range(100)
    .map(function(i) {
        return Math.random() * 30;
    })
    .map(function(d, i) {
            return { X: i * 10, Y: d }
    });
```

The path is generated using a `d3.svg.area()` object:

```
var generator = d3.svg.area()
    .y0(100)
    .x(function(d) { return d.X; })
    .y1(function (d) { return d.Y; });
```

An area path generator requires providing three accessor functions:

- `x()`: This specifies where to get the X values
- `y0()`: This gets the position of the baseline of the area
- `y1()`: This retrieves the height at the given `x()` value

The actual SVG path is then created and styled similar to the previous example.

Creating arcs, donuts, wedges, and segments

An arc is a slice of a circle that has a portion of it swept through two specific angles. An arc swept through a full 360 degrees will actually result in a circle. A sweep of less than 360 degrees gives you a wedge of that circle and is often called a pie **wedge**.

An arc is created using the `d3.svg.arc()` function. This generator takes four parameters, describing the mathematics of the arc. The size of the wedge is defined by using the `.outerRadius()` function and an inner radius that is specified using `.innerRadius()`.

The following example uses an arc to draw a circle:

bl.ock (9.3): `http://goo.gl/fJN80J`

The code to create the generator is the following:

```
var generator = d3.svg.arc()
    .innerRadius(0)
    .outerRadius(60)
    .startAngle(0)
    .endAngle(Math.PI * 2);
```

The generator specifies an inner radius of 0 and outer radius of 60. The start and end angles are in radians and sweep out an entire circle.

The following example increases the size of the inner radius to create a donut:

bl.ock (9.4): http://goo.gl/NDVPRw

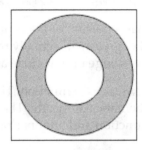

The only difference in the code is the call to .innerRadius():

```
var generator = d3.svg.arc()
    .innerRadius(30)
    .outerRadius(60)
    .startAngle(0)
    .endAngle(Math.PI * 2);
```

We have now created a donut! Now how about an example of creating a pie wedge? We can create a pie wedge by specifying an inner radius of 0 and setting the start angle and end angle to not sweep out a full 360 degrees, as shown in the following example.

To demonstrate, the following example creates a pie wedge sweeping between 45 and 105 degrees:

bl.ock (9.5): http://goo.gl/cNizYk

The generator for the preceding pie wedge is as follows:

```
var generator = d3.svg.arc()
    .innerRadius(0)
    .outerRadius(60)
    .startAngle(45 * Math.PI * 2 / 360)
    .endAngle(105 * Math.PI * 2 / 360);
```

A final example for arcs is to create a segment by increasing the inner radius of the previous example to be greater than 0:

bl.ock (9.6): `http://goo.gl/24djAS`

```
var generator = d3.svg.arc()
    .innerRadius(40)
    .outerRadius(60)
    .startAngle(45 * Math.PI * 2/360)
    .endAngle(105 * Math.PI * 2/360);
```

Creating a pie chart

One of the most common type of charts is the pie chart (it is also one of the most reviled). A pie chart could be created by using multiple arc generators and placing them manually.

To make this simpler, D3.js provides us with a tool to help us generate pies and the associated arcs with a generator for pies, `d3.layout.pie()`. From an array of data, this function will generate an array of arc specifications that we can then use to generate all the pie segments automatically.

So, let's examine the creation of a pie:

bl.ock (9.7): `http://goo.gl/omVW2n`

The preceding code results in the following pie chart:

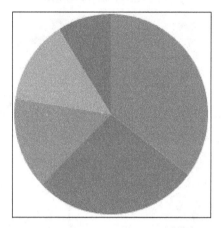

The example starts by declaring values that represent each piece of the pie and then we pass that to the `d3.layout.pie()` function:

```
var data = [21, 32, 35, 64, 83];
var pieSegments = d3.layout.pie()(data);
```

If you examine the contents of `pieSegments`, you will see a series of objects similar to the following:

```
[[object Object] {
   data: 21,
   endAngle: 6.283185307179587,
   padAngle: 0,
   startAngle: 5.721709173346517,
   value: 21
},
   ...
]
```

We can use this data via an arc generator and generate the pie:

```
var arcGenerator = d3.svg.arc()
    .innerRadius(0)
    .outerRadius(100)
    .startAngle(function(d) {
        return d.startAngle;
    })
    .endAngle(function(d) {
        return d.endAngle;
    });
var colors = d3.scale.category10();
group.selectAll('path')
    .data(pieSegments)
    .enter()
    .append('path')
    .attr('d', arcGenerator)
    .style('fill', function(d, i) {
        return colors(i);
    });
```

Exploding the pie

We can make an exploded pie by setting the width of the border of the pie wedges. The following example demonstrates this in action. We'll skip the walkthrough of the code, as it's just adding a `stroke` and `stroke-width` to the previous example:

bl.ock (9.8): `http://goo.gl/fhQEau`

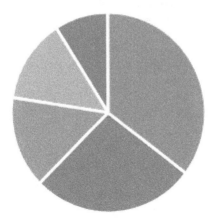

Creating a ring graph

We can also easily make this into a ring chart by increasing the inner radius, as shown in the following example (with a brief modification to the previous example):

bl.ock (9.9): `http://goo.gl/Mk60ws`

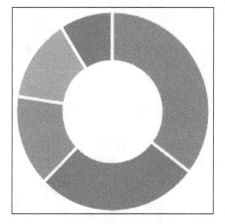

Creating symbols

Symbols are little shapes that can be used on a chart, much like how we used small circles and squares in the chapter on scatter plots. D3.js comes with a generator that creates six symbols: circle, cross, diamond, square, triangle-down, and triangle-up.

These symbols are named, and the `d3.svg.symbolTypes` contains an array of the names of the available symbol types. A symbol is then created by passing the symbol name to the `d3.svg.symbol().type()` function, which returns a path generator for the specified symbol.

An example of rendering the available symbols is available at the following link:

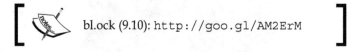

bl.ock (9.10): `http://goo.gl/AM2ErM`

The preceding code renders the following symbols as the result:

Perhaps they're not the most exciting things in the world, but they are useful for representing different data items on scatter plots or as point markers on line diagrams.

Using diagonals to create curved lines

The diagonal is one of my personal favorites, and it can be used in many complex visualizations. This is a concept which I believe is best understood by seeing an example:

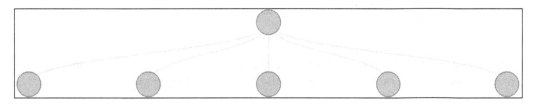

The diagonal generator generates the curved lines between one point and a set of other points, generating the appropriate curves based on the position of the target points.

The following example creates the previous image:

bl.ock (9.11): http://goo.gl/by9B4S

This example starts with defining the source and target positions using JavaScript objects, and then, by creating from those an array of objects representing every combination of source and target:

```
var source = { x: 500, y: 50 };
var targets = [
    { x: 100, y: 150 },
    { x: 300, y: 150 },
    { x: 500, y: 150 },
    { x: 700, y: 150 },
    { x: 900, y: 150 }
];
var links = targets.map(function (target) {
    return { source: source, target: target };
});
```

We can then generate the curved lines using the following selection, which uses a
`d3.svg.diagonal()` object as the generator of the path data:

```
svg.selectAll('path')
    .data(links)
    .enter()
    .append('path')
    .attr({
        d: d3.svg.diagonal(),
        fill: 'none',
        stroke: '#ccc'
    });
```

The circles are not rendered by the diagonal generator. The code renders and
positions them based on the positions of the source and target points.

Drawing line graphs using interpolators

Now let's examine creating line graphs using a number of the built-in line
generators. The capability for rendering lines in D3.js is very robust, and can be used
to generate lines with straight segments, or to fit curves through a series of points
using a number of different algorithms.

When rendering a line using a line generator, D3.js applies an interpolator across
your data to determine how to create the path segments that connect your data
points. The following tables lists the available line interpolators that are available:

Interpolator	Operation
linear	Straight lines between points
linear-closed	Closes the line segment, last point to first, making a polygon
step-before	Step-wise drawing vertically then horizontally
step-after	Step-wise drawing horizontally then vertically
basis	Renders a b-spline curve with control points at the ends
basis-open	Renders a b-spline curve with control points at the ends, not closing the loop
basic-closed	Renders a b-spline curve with control points at the ends, closing the loop
bundle	Equivalent to basis, but with a tension parameter
cardinal	A cardinal spline, with control points at the ends

Interpolator	Operation
`cardinal-open`	A cardinal spline, with control points at the ends; the line may not intersect the end points, but will pass through the internal points
`cardinal-closed`	Closes the cardinal spline into a loop
`monotone`	A cubic interpolation that preserves monotonicity in y

The default is to use a linear interpolator, which essentially draws a straight line between each pair of adjacent points. We will take a look at each of these, as I think they are worth demonstrating (and are fun!).

The example is available at the following link:

bl.ock (9.12): `http://goo.gl/MdjuPz`

The application presents the user with two options. One is to select the type of interpolation and the other is to select a tension value, which is only used when the selected interpolation is bundle.

The example then generates a cycle of a sine wave that is represented by 8 points. As an example, the result is the following when linear interpolation is selected:

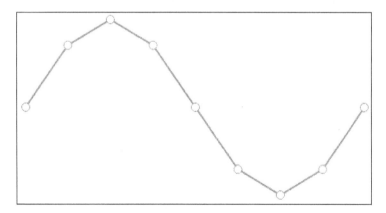

The application starts by creating the dropdown boxes and the main SVG element in HTML. It then sets up the scales for the sine wave to map the points into the SVG. The first time the page is loaded, and upon every change of a selection for interpolation or tension, the `redraw()` function is called and the graph is generated.

The `redraw()` function retrieves the current value from the interpolation dropdown and uses it to create the line path generator using the selected value:

```
var line = d3.svg.line()
    .interpolate(interpolation)
    .x(function(d) { return xScale(d[0]); })
    .y(function(d) { return yScale(d[1]); });
```

If the selected interpolation is bundle, it also retrieves the selected value for the tension and applies that value to the line path generator:

```
if (interpolation === "bundle") {
    var tensionsSel = document.getElementById('tensions');
    var tension = tensionsSel.options[
        tensionsSel.selectedIndex].value;
    line.tension(tension);
}
```

The lines are then generated using a path and the associated generator and then circles are added at the location of each point.

Now let's examine what each of these interpolations does to render our sine wave.

Linear and linear-closed interpolators

The linear interpolator draws straight lines between the points:

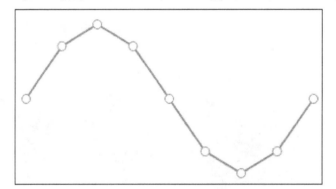

Linear closed is a slight variant that also connects the last point to the first:

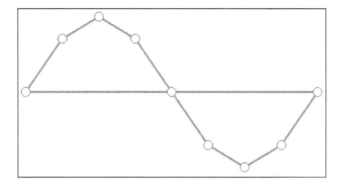

Step-before and step-after interpolations

The best way to demonstrate a step-before and step-after is just by giving examples. But essentially, each pair of points are connected by two lines, one horizontal and the other vertical.

With step-before, the vertical line come first:

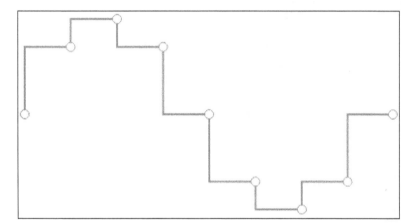

A step-after renders the horizontal line first:

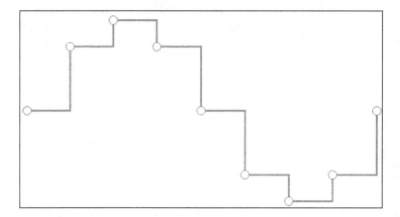

Creating curved lines using the basis interpolation

A **basis** curve will pass through the end points but may not pass through internal points. The internal points influence the curve of the line, but it is not necessary that the line runs through any of the internal points.

The following is an example of the basis interpolation:

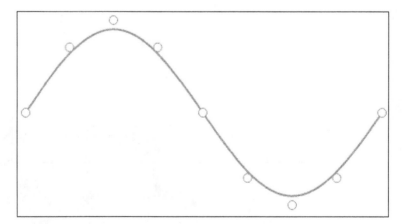

A **basis-open** interpolation does not pass through the end points. It looks similar to basis, but with the line not being drawn between the first and second points and between the next to last and last points:

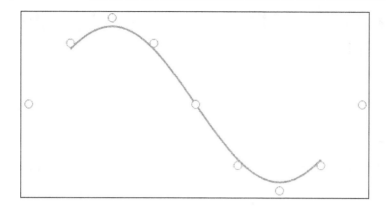

Why would we want this? This would be in the case where the first and last are control points and can be changed in the X and Y values to influence how the curve moves through the inner points. Examining this is beyond the scope of this book, but I challenge you to take the concepts that you learned in *Chapter 8, Adding User Interactivity*, allowing the user to drag the control points around, and see how that changes the flow of the line.

basis-closed tells the generator to close the loop and ensure the loop is smooth across all points (the small change in code is omitted again). The result is the following:

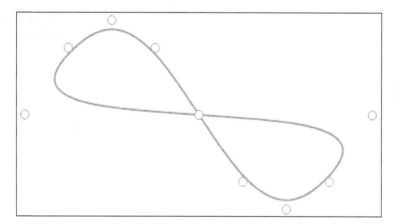

Pretty awesome! As you can see, you can use these interpolators to create really complex curved shapes. Imagine doing this by creating the path commands all by yourself. I dare you to examine the path commands for this line—there are a lot of them.

Creating curved lines using the bundle interpolation

bundle is similar to basis, except you can specify a parameter for the amount of tension in the line that is generated. Tension allows you to control how tightly the line will conform to the given points. To specify tension, chain the .tension() function with a parameter value between 0.0 and 1.0 (the default is 0.7). The following shows a selected tension of 0.75:

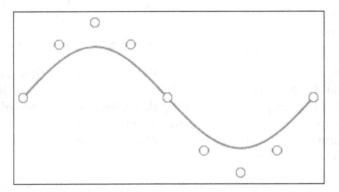

You can see how the generated line (well, curve) is now influenced a lot less closely by the points. If you set the value to 0.0, this would actually be a straight line. To demonstrate efficiently other values for tension, the following table demonstrates the change in shape at various points of tension from 0.0 to 1.0:

Tension	Result
0.0	

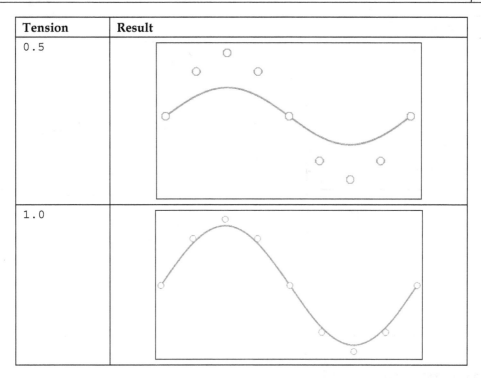

Tension	Result
0.5	
1.0	

If you compare a tension of 1.0 to the basis interpolation, you will notice they are identical.

Creating curved lines using the cardinal interpolation

cardinal curves are like basis curves, except that the lines are forced to run through all points. The following graph demonstrates the normal, open, and closed forms:

Interpolation	Result
cardinal	

Interpolation	Result
cardinal-open	
cardinal-closed	

Summary

In this chapter, we examined several techniques of creating complex shapes using D3.js path data generators. We started with examples of common generators, including line, area, circles, donuts, arcs, and diagonals. These are extremely powerful tools and enhance your ability to create complex visualizations easily.

We finished the chapter with an examination of line interpolators, a means of informing the line path generator of how to fit lines between data points. These interpolations, including the default linear interpolation, are for the basis of efficiently creating complex line graphs and curved shapes that fit data.

In the next chapter on layouts, we will move a little higher up the visual stack of D3.js to examine layouts, which are essentially generators for complex data visualizations.

10
Using Layouts to Visualize Series and Hierarchical Data

We are now going to get into what some refer to as the most powerful features of D3.js —layouts. Layouts encapsulate algorithms that examine your data and calculate the positions for visual elements for specific type of graphs such as bars, areas, bubbles, chords, trees, and many others.

We will dive into several useful layouts. These will be categorized into several main categories based upon the structure of the data and type of visualization such as stacked, hierarchical, chords, and flow-based diagrams. For each of the categories, we will go over creating a number of examples, complete with data and code.

Specifically, we will examine creating the following types of graphs and layouts:

- Stacked layouts to create bar and area graphs
- Hierarchical diagrams including trees, cluster dendrograms, and enclosures
- Relationships between items using chord diagrams
- Flowing data using streamgraphs and Sankey diagrams

Using stacked layouts

Stacks are a class of layouts that take multiple series of data, where each measurement from each series is rendered atop each other. These are suited for demonstrating the comparative size of the measurements from each series at each measurement. They are also great at demonstrating how the multiple streams of data change over the entire set of measurements.

Stacked diagrams basically come down to two different representations: stacked bar graphs and stacked area graphs. We will examine both of these and explain how to create these with D3.js.

Creating a stacked bar graph

The implementation of a stacked bar graph is similar to that of a bar graph, except that we need to take into account the fact that the height of each bar consists of the sum of each measurement. Normally, each bar is subdivided, with each division sized relative to the sum, and is given a different color to differentiate it.

Let's jump into creating our own stacked bar graph. The data that will be used can be found at `https://goo.gl/6fJrxE`.

The following are the first few lines of the file. This data represents seven series of data, each series a specific range of age, broken down categorically by state. Each value represents the population for the given state in that age group.

```
State,Under 5 Years,5 to 13 Years,14 to 17 Years,18 to 24 Years,25 to
44 Years,45 to 64 Years,65 Years and Over
AL,310504,552339,259034,450818,1231572,1215966,641667
AK,52083,85640,42153,74257,198724,183159,50277
AZ,515910,828669,362642,601943,1804762,1523681,862573
```

The online example is available at the following link:

bl.ock (10.1): `http://goo.gl/G3BIL7`

The resulting bar graph is the following:

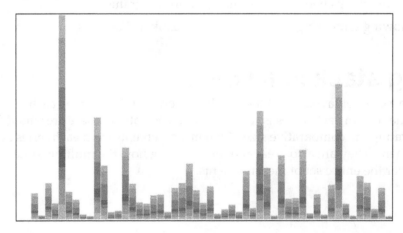

The data is loaded using `d3.csv()`:

```
var url = 'https://gist.githubusercontent.com/
d3byex/25129228aa50c30ef01f/raw/17838a0a03d94328a529de1dd768e956ce217
af1/stacked_bars.csv';
d3.csv(url, function (error, data) {
```

Examining the first object in the resulting data, we see the following structure:

```
▼0: Object
    5 to 13 Years: "552339"
    14 to 17 Years: "259034"
    18 to 24 Years: "450818"
    25 to 44 Years: "1231572"
    45 to 64 Years: "1215966"
    65 Years and Over: "641667"
    State: "AL"
    Under 5 Years: "310504"
```

This array has 51 elements, one for each state of the US and Washington D.C. This data needs to be converted into a structure that gives us information for rendering each bar and the rectangle for each series within each of the bars. To do this, we need to go through three steps, the last one culminating with the use of `d3.layout.stack()`.

First, the code extracts the unique keys for each series of data, which is the age groups. This can be retrieved by filtering out all properties of each object in the array where the property name is not equal to `State`.

```
var keys = d3.keys(data[0])
    .filter(function (key) {
        return key !== "State";
    });
```

```
["Under 5 Years", "5 to 13 Years", "14 to 17 Years", "18 to 24 Years", "25 to 44 Years",
"45 to 64 Years", "65 Years and Over"]
```

Using these keys, we can reorganize the data so that we have an array representing the values for each age group:

```
var statesAndAges = keys.map(function (ageRange) {
    return data.map(function (d) {
```

```
        return {
            x: d.State,
            y: +d[ageRange]
        };
    });
});
```

The `statesAndAges` variables now is a seven-element array, with each element being an array of objects representing the x and y values for each series:

```
▼ [Array[51], Array[51], Array[51], Array[51], Array[51], Array[51], Array[51]]
  ▼ 0: Array[51]
    ▼ 0: Object
        x: "AL"
        y: 310504
      ▶ __proto__: Object
    ▼ 1: Object
        x: "AK"
        y: 52083
      ▶ __proto__: Object
```

Now, using these keys, we create a `d3.layout.stack()` function and have it process this data.

```
var stackedData = d3.layout.stack()(statesAndAges);
```

The result of the stacking of this data is that the stack function will add an additional property, y0, to each object in each series. The value of y0 will be the value of the sum of the y values in the previously lower-numbered series. To demonstrate, the following are the values of the objects in the first object of each array:

```
Object {x: "AL", y: 310504, y0: 0}
Object {x: "AL", y: 552339, y0: 310504}
Object {x: "AL", y: 259034, y0: 862843}
Object {x: "AL", y: 450818, y0: 1121877}
Object {x: "AL", y: 1231572, y0: 1572695}
Object {x: "AL", y: 1215966, y0: 2804267}
Object {x: "AL", y: 641667, y0: 4020233}
```

The value of y0 in the first object is 0. The value of y0 in the second is 310504, which is equal to y0 + y of the first object. The value of y0 in the third object is y0 + y of the second, or 862843. This function has stacked the y values, with each y value being the value of y for the individual segment of the bar that will be rendered.

The data is now organized to render the bar graph. The next step is to create the main SVG element:

```
var width = 960, height = 500;
var svg = d3.select('body')
    .append("svg")
    .attr({
        width: width,
        height: height
    });
```

The code next calculates the x and y scales to map the bars into the specified number of pixels. The y scale will have a domain that ranges from 0 to the maximum sum of y0 and y within all the series:

```
var yScale = d3.scale.linear()
        .domain([0,
            d3.max(stackedData, function (d) {
                return d3.max(d, function (d) {
                    return d.y0 + d.y;
                });
            })
        ])
        .range([0, height]);
```

The x scale is set up as an ordinal rangeRoundBands, one for each state:

```
var xScale = d3.scale.ordinal()
    .domain(d3.range(stackedData[0].length))
    .rangeRoundBands([0, width], 0.05);
```

The code then creates a group for each of the series, assigning to each the color that the rectangles within will be filled with:

```
var colors = d3.scale.ordinal()
    .range(["#98abc5", "#8a89a6", "#7b6888",
        "#6b486b", "#a05d56", "#d0743c", "#ff8c00"]);
```

```
var groups = svg.selectAll("g")
    .data(stackedData)
    .enter()
    .append("g")
    .style("fill", function (d, i) {
        return colors(i);
    });
```

The last step is to render all the rectangles. The following performs this by creating 51 rectangles within each group:

```
groups.selectAll("rect")
    .data(function (d) { return d; })
    .enter()
    .append("rect")
    .attr("x", function (d, i) {
        return xScale(i);
    })
    .attr("y", function (d, i) {
        return height - yScale(d.y) - yScale(d.y0);
    })
    .attr("height", function (d) {
        return yScale(d.y);
    })
    .attr("width", xScale.rangeBand());
});
```

That's it! You have drawn this graph using this data.

Modifying the stacked bar into a stacked area graph

Stacked area graphs give a different view of the data than a stacked bar does. To create a stacked area graph, we change the rendering of each series of data as a path. The path is defined using an area generator, which has the y values on the lower end and the sum of y0 + y on the upper end.

The code for the stacked area graph is available online at the following link:

bl.ock (10.2): http://goo.gl/PRw8wv

The resulting output from this example is the following:

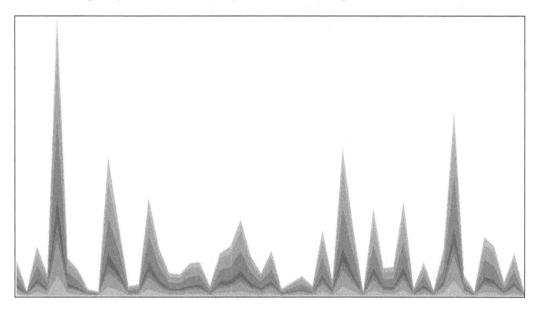

The change from the previous example is relatively small. The data is loaded and organized exactly the same. The scales and colors are also created the same way.

The difference comes in the rendering of the visuals. Instead of groups of rectangles, we render a filled path for each series. The following creates these paths and assigns the color for each:

```
svg.selectAll("path")
    .data(stackedData)
    .enter()
    .append("path")
    .style("fill", function (d, i) {
        return colors(i);
    });
```

This has generated the path elements, but has not assigned the path's d property yet to create the actual path data. That's our next step, but we first need to create an area generator to convert our data to that which is needed for the path. This area generator needs to have three values specified, the x value, y0 (which represents the bottom of the area), and y1 (which is at the top of the area):

```
var area = d3.svg.area()
    .x(function (d, i) {
        return xScale(i);
    })
    .y0(function (d) {
        return height - yScale(d.y0);
    })
    .y1(function (d) {
        return height - yScale(d.y + d.y0);
    });
```

And finally, we select the paths we just created and bind to each the appropriate series, setting the d attribute of the corresponding path to the result of calling the area generator. Note that this calls the area generator for each series:

```
svg.selectAll("path")
    .data(stackedData)
    .transition()
    .attr("d", function (d) {
        return area(d);
    });
```

Converting the area graph to an expanded area graph

There is a variant of a stacked area graph known as an expanded area graph. An expanded area graph fills the entire area of the graph completely and can be used to easily visualize the relative percentage that each series represents at each point.

This type of graph is created from a stacked area graph by normalizing the data at each point across all series to 1.0. The following example demonstrates how this is performed:

bl.ock (10.3): `http://goo.gl/g9BH4L`

The resulting graph is the following:

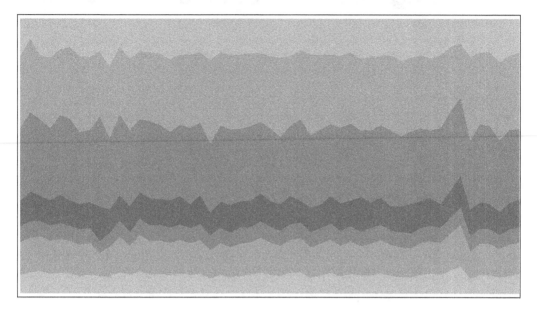

This visually gives us a good feel of how the relative size of each age group changes during the period. For the most part, the age groups have stayed at the same proportion, except for perhaps one state near the end of the data.

It's a really easy thing to convert the stacked area graph to an expanded area graph. To accomplish this, we need to do two things. The first of these is to change how we stack the data. We change the stack operation to the following:

```
var stackedData = d3.layout.stack()
    .offset('expand')(statesAndAges);
```

The change here is to add a call to `.offset("expand")`. This informs D3.js to normalize the results to `[0, 1]` for each point. The default offset is `"zero"`, which, as we have seen, starts Y values at `0` and does a running sum.

The data is now ready, and the second change is to change the Y scale to the account for the domain as `[0, 1]`:

```
var yScale = d3.scale.linear()
    .domain([0, 1])
    .range([0, height]);
```

You now have your expanded area graph.

Visualizing hierarchical data

Hierarchal layouts display information that is hierarchical in nature. That is perhaps a slightly recursive definition, but the basic idea is that certain data items break down into zero or more data items at a lower level, and then perhaps to another level, and so on, for as many levels as is required.

Hierarchical layouts are all created from the d3.layout.hierarchy() function, but there are specializations of this function that create various layouts which fall into common visual patterns such as trees, clusters, and enclosures and packs. We will take a look at an example of each of these types of layouts.

Tree diagrams

Tree diagrams are essentially node-link diagrams. In *Chapter 9, Complex Shapes using Paths*, we saw the use of a path generator known as a diagonal. This generator was able to create curved line segments that can connect a node to one or more nodes. To refresh you, we had an example that generated the following:

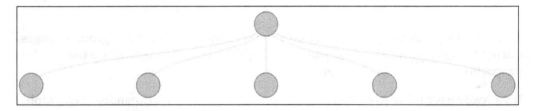

This is a basic node-link diagram. Tree diagrams utilize diagonals and apply them to many levels of hierarchy. The diagram can be structured as a tree or in other more complex layouts such as a radial cluster (which we will examine). The layouts will calculate the positions of the nodes and then we need to render the nodes and the attached diagonals.

We will start by creating a simple tree diagram. The data is available at `https://goo.gl/mcdT9r`. The contents of the data are the following:

```
{
    "name": "Mike and Marcia",
    "children": [
      {
        "name": "Children",
        "children": [
          { "name": "Mikael" }
        ]
      },
      {
        "name": "Pets",
        "children": [
          {
            "name": "Dogs",
            "children": [
              { "name": "Bleu" },
              { "name": "Tagg" }
            ]
          },
          {
            "name": "Cats",
            "children": [
              { "name": "Bob" },
              { "name": "Peanut" }
            ]
          }
        ]
      }
    ]
}
```

The example is available at the following location:

bl.ock (10.4): `http://goo.gl/t1hBTS`

The result of the rendering is the following tree diagram:

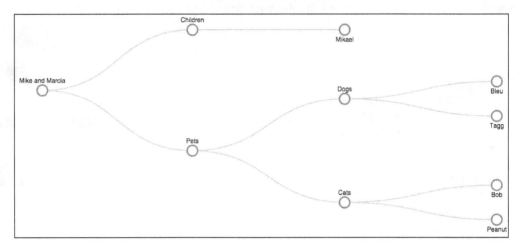

Our example begins with loading the data, establishing metrics for the diagram, creating the main SVG element, and establishing a main group and margins:

```
var url = 'https://gist.githubusercontent.
com/d3byex/25129228aa50c30ef01f/raw/
c1c3ad9fa745c42c5410fba29cefccac47cd0ec7/familytree.json';
d3.json(url, function (error, data) {
    var width = 960, height = 500,
        nodeRadius = 10,
        margin = {
            left: 50, top: 10,
            bottom: 10, right: 40
        };

    var svg = d3.select('body')
        .append("svg")
        .attr({
            width: width,
            height: height
        });
    var mainGroup = svg.append("g")
        .attr("transform", "translate(" + margin.left + "," +
                                        margin.top + ')');
```

To convert the data into a visual representation of a tree, we will create a tree layout using the d3.layout.tree() function.

```
var tree = d3.layout.tree()
    .size([
        height - (margin.bottom + margin.top),
        width - (margin.left + margin.right),
    ]);
```

This informs D3.js that we want to create a tree that will map its data into a rectangle specified by height and width. Notice that the height is specified before width.

There are two visual components to the graph: the nodes, represented by circles, and the edges, which are diagonals. To calculate the nodes, we use the .nodes() function of the layout and pass it our data.

```
var nodes = tree.nodes(data);
```

The tree function looks for a top-level node with a children property. It will traverse all the nodes in the hierarchy and determine its depth, which, in this case, has four levels. It will then add x and y properties to each node, where these represent the calculated position of the nodes based upon the layout and the specific width and height.

Examining the contents of the nodes variable, we can see that D3.js has given us the positions for each node (the following shows the first two nodes):

```
▼ [Object, Object, Object, Object, Object, Object, Object, Object, Object, Object]
  ▼ 0: Object
    ▶ children: Array[2]
      depth: 0
      name: "Mike and Marcia"
      x: 176
      y: 0
    ▶ __proto__: Object
  ▼ 1: Object
    ▶ children: Array[1]
      depth: 1
      name: "Children"
    ▶ parent: Object
      x: 64
      y: 290
```

To get the links in the tree, we call `tree.links(nodes)`:

```
var links = tree.links(nodes);
```

The following shows the link that results in this example:

```
▼ [Object, Object, Object, Object, Object, Object, Object, Object, Object]
  ▼ 0: Object
    ▼ source: Object
      ▶ children: Array[2]
        depth: 0
        name: "Mike and Marcia"
        x: 176
        y: 0
      ▶ __proto__: Object
    ▼ target: Object
      ▶ children: Array[1]
        depth: 1
        name: "Children"
      ▶ parent: Object
        x: 64
        y: 290
      ▶ __proto__: Object
    ▶ __proto__: Object
```

The newly created data structure consists of an element for each link, of which each object contains a `source` and `target` property that points to the node that is on each end of the link.

We now have our data ready for creating visuals. Next is the statement for creating the generator for the diagonals. We use the `.projection()` function, since we need to tell the generator how to find the x and y value from each datum:

```
var diagonal = d3.svg.diagonal()
    .projection(function(d) {
        return [d.y, d.x];
    });
```

Now we can create the diagonals, reusing the generator for each. The diagonals are created before the nodes, because we want the nodes to be in front:

```
mainGroup.selectAll('path')
    .data(links)
    .enter()
    .append('path', 'g')
    .attr({
        d: diagonal,
        fill: 'none',
        stroke: '#ccc',
        'stroke-width': 2
    });
```

Now the code creates the circles and the labels. We will represent each node with a group containing a circle and a piece of text. The following creates these groups and places them at the calculated locations:

```
var circleGroups = mainGroup.selectAll('g')
    .data(nodes)
    .enter()
    .append('g')
    .attr('transform', function (d) {
        return 'translate(' + d.y + ',' + d.x + ')';
    });
```

Next, we add the circles as a child of each node's group element:

```
circleGroups.append('circle')
    .attr({
        r: nodeRadius,
        fill: '#fff',
        stroke: 'steelblue',
        'stroke-width': 3,
    });
```

And then we add the text for the node label to the group:

```
circleGroups.append('text')
    .text(function (d) {
        return d.name;
    })
    .attr('y', function (d) {
        return d.children || d._children ?
            -nodeRadius * 2 : nodeRadius * 2;
    })
    .attr({
        dy: '.35em',
        'text-anchor': 'middle',
        'fill-opacity': 1
    })
    .style('font', '12px sans-serif');
```

The function, when assigning the y attribute, offsets the position of the text to be above the circle if the node is not a leaf and underneath the node if it is a leaf node.

Creating a cluster dendrogram

A hierarchy can also be visualized as a variant of a tree known as a **cluster dendrogram**. A cluster dendrogram differs from a tree graph in that we use a cluster layout. This layout places the root of the tree at the center. The depth of the data is calculated, and that number of levels of concentric circles are fit into the diagram. The nodes for each level of depth are then placed around the edge of the circle for their respective depth.

To demonstrate this, we will utilize the data available at https://goo.gl/t3M7n1. This data represents three levels of data, with one root node and four nodes on the second level; each of those nodes has nine children.

The following is a sample of the data:

```
{
    "name": "1",
    "children": [
        {
            "name": "1-1",
            "children": [
                { "name": "1-1-1" },
                { "name": "1-1-2" },
                { "name": "1-1-3" },
```

```
            { "name": "1-1-4" },
            { "name": "1-1-5" },
            { "name": "1-1-6" },
            { "name": "1-1-7" },
            { "name": "1-1-8" },
            { "name": "1-1-9" }
        ]
    },
    {
        "name": "1-2",
        "children": [
            { "name": "1-2-1" },
            { "name": "1-2-2" },
            { "name": "1-2-3" },
...
```

The example is available at the following location:

bl.ock (10.5): http://goo.gl/cQtPuH

The resulting graph is the following:

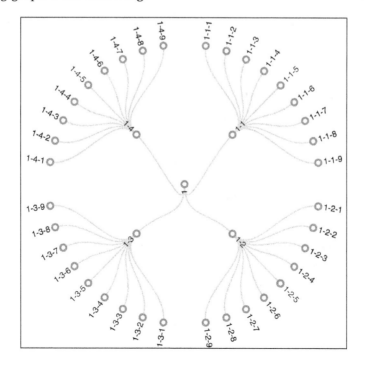

Let's step through how this is created. The code is similar to the tree example, but with some differences. After the data is loaded, the main SVG element is created, and then a group is placed within the element:

```
var center = width / 2;
var mainGroup = svg.append('g')
    .attr("transform", "translate(" + center + "," +
                                      center + ")");
```

The layout algorithm will calculate the points around a center at **(0, 0)**, so we center the group to center the graph.

The layout is then created using `d3.layout.cluster()`:

```
var cluster = d3.layout.cluster()
    .size([
        360,
        center - 50
    ]);
```

The size specifies two things; the first parameter is the number of degrees that the points will sweep through on the outer circle. This specifies `360` degrees so that we completely fill the outer circle. The second parameter is the tree depth, or what is essentially the radius of the outermost circle.

Next, we use the layout to calculate the position for the nodes and links:

```
var nodes = cluster.nodes(data);
var links = cluster.links(nodes);
```

It is worth examining the first few nodes that result from these calculations:

```
▼ [Object, Object, Object, Object, Object, Object, Object, Object, Object, Object, Object, Object, Object, Object, Object,
Object, Object, Object, Object, Object, Object, Object, Object, Object, Object, Object, Object, Object, Object, Object,
Object, Object, Object, Object, Object, Object, Object, Object, Object, Object, Object]
  ▼ 0: Object
    ▶ children: Array[4]
      depth: 0
      name: "1"
      x: 180
      y: 0
    ▶ __proto__: Object
  ▼ 1: Object
    ▶ children: Array[9]
      depth: 1
      name: "1-1"
    ▶ parent: Object
      x: 45
      y: 100
    ▶ __proto__: Object
  ▼ 2: Object
      depth: 2
      name: "1-1-1"
    ▶ parent: Object
      x: 9
      y: 200
    ▶ __proto__: Object
```

The x and y properties specify a direction and distance at which the node (and edges) is to be placed. The x property specifies the angle from vertical, and the value of the y property specifies the distance.

The diagonals are calculated using a radial diagonal, which needs to convert the x values into radians:

```
var diagonal = d3.svg.diagonal.radial()
    .projection(function(d) {
        return [
              d.y,
              d.x / 180 * Math.PI
        ];
    });
```

Now we can use this radial generator diagonal that connects the nodes:

```
mainGroup.selectAll('path')
    .data(links)
    .enter()
    .append('path')
    .attr({
        'd': diagonal,
        fill: 'none',
        stroke: '#ccc',
        'stroke-width': 2
    });
```

Next, we create a group to hold the node and the text. The trick to this is that we need to translate and rotate the group into the correct position:

```
var nodeGroups = mainGroup.selectAll("g")
    .data(nodes)
    .enter()
    .append("g")
    .attr("transform", function(d) {
        return "rotate(" + (d.x - 90) + ")translate(" + d.y + ")";
    });
```

We rotate the group by 90 degrees from the calculated angle. This changes the orientation of the the text to flow out from the circle, along the diagonals. Note that rotate works in degrees, not radians, as was required for the radial generator. The translate uses just the y value, which moves the group out that distance along the specified angle. Now we add the circles to the group:

```
nodeGroups.append("circle")
    .attr({
        r: nodeRadius,
        fill: '#fff',
        stroke: 'steelblue',
        'stroke-width': 3
    });
```

And finally, we add the text. Note the small calculation around the text being at an angle greater or less than 180 degrees. This essentially says that nodes on the left-half of the diagram are positioned with the end of the text against the node and on the right side, start at the beginning of the text. The text is also transformed by twice the circle radius to prevent it from overlapping the circle:

```
nodeGroups.append('text')
    .attr({
        dy: '.31em',
        'text-anchor': function(d) {
            return d.x < 180 ? 'start' : 'end';
        },
        'transform': function(d) {
            return d.x < 180 ?
                            'translate(' + (nodeRadius*2) + ')' :
                            'rotate(180)' +
                            'translate(' + (-nodeRadius*2) + ')';
        }
    })
    .style('font', '12px sans-serif')
    .text(function(d) { return d.name; });
```

Representing hierarchy with an enclosure diagram

Enclosure diagrams use nesting of visuals to represent the hierarchy. The size of each leaf node's circle reveals a quantitative dimension of each data point. The enclosing circles show the approximate cumulative size of each subtree, but note that because of wasted space, there is some distortion between levels. Therefore, only the leaf nodes can be compared accurately.

The following is the location of the online example:

The following image is the resulting visual:

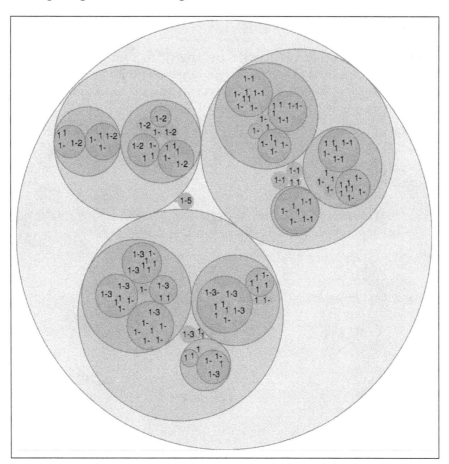

The data used by the example is available at `https://goo.gl/RzvlV3`. It is similar in structure to the data in the previous example, except that a `value` property is added to each node. The values of the leaf nodes are summed in their parents, repeating all the way to the top.

Essentially, this data is a rollup of the values, much like what would be performed when rolling up sales numbers from sales persons, to offices, to divisions, to the corporate level. The diagram then allows us to see relative sizes of the numbers in the leaf nodes, which are colored orange, and then get an idea of the total at each level up the tree.

Now let's examine how this is created. The example begins with loading of the data and then creating an SVG element of a specified diameter. Then, a pack layout is created that is also used the diameter. The hierarchical bubbles that are created will be measured to fit within the specified diameter:

```
var pack = d3.layout.pack()
    .size([diameter, diameter])
    .value(function (d) { return d.value; });
```

Now we render the circles. For each node, we append a group that is translated to the appropriate position and then a circle is appended with its radius set to the calculated radius (`d.r`), the `fill`, `fill-opacity`, and the `stroke` to different values depending on whether the node is a leaf or not:

```
var nodes = svg.datum(data)
    .selectAll('g')
    .data(pack.nodes)
    .enter()
    .append('g')
    .attr('transform', function (d) {
        return 'translate(' + d.x + ',' + d.y + ')';
    });

nodes.append('circle')
    .each(function (d) {
        d3.select(this)
            .attr({
```

```
            r: d.r,
            fill: d.children ? 'rgb(31, 119, 180)' :
                                '#ff7f0e',
            'fill-opacity': d.children ? 0.25 : 1.0,
            stroke: d.children ? 'rgb(31, 119, 180)' : 'none'
        });
    });
```

The last step is to add the text to the leaf circles (the ones without children, as specified using the filter):

```
nodes.filter(function(d) {
        return !d.children;
    })
    .append('text')
    .attr('dy', '.3em')
    .style({
        'text-anchor': 'middle',
        'font': '10px sans-serif'
    })
    .text(function(d) {
        return d.name.substring(0, d.r / 3);
    });
```

Representing relationships with chord diagrams

Chord diagrams demonstrate the relationships among a group of entities. To demonstrate, we will use the example available at the following link:

bl.ock (10.7): http://goo.gl/8mRDSg

The resulting diagram is the following:

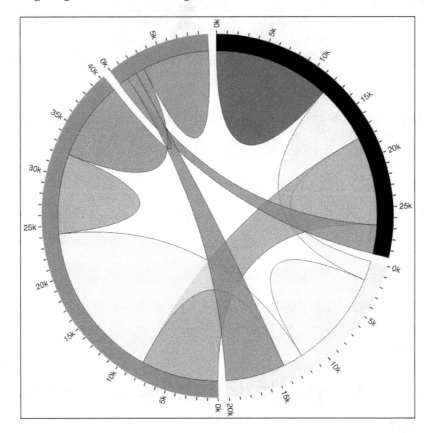

The data in this example is a square matrix of data, with rows and columns representing hair color (black, blonde, brown, and red). The data represents a total sample of **100000** measurements, where each row demonstrates the total count of the other hair colors which a person of a given hair color prefers:

Has	*Prefers*				
	Black	**Blonde**	**Brown**	**Red**	**Total**
Black	11975	5871	8916	2868	29630
Blonde	1951	10048	2060	6171	20230
Brown	8010	16145	8090	8045	40290
Red	1013	990	940	6907	9850
Total	22949	30354	20006	23991	10000

To explain the diagram, each outer ring segment represents the number of people that have a given hair color. The size of these ring segments is relative to the percentage of people of a given hair color. Each arc from a given color ring segment to another ring segment (or itself) represents the number of people of that hair color that prefer the hair color on the other side of that arc and vice versa. The ticks on the outside of each ring segment gives a feel for the total number of the people represented.

Now let's step through creating this graph. First, we create our top-level SVG elements. The main group is translated to the center, as the positions will be centered around (0, 0):

```
var width = 960, height = 500;
var svg = d3.select('body')
    .append('svg')
    .attr({
        width: width,
        height: height
    });
var mainGroup = svg.append('g')
    .attr('transform', 'translate(' + width / 2 + ',' +
                                      height / 2 + ')');
```

Now let's declare the data. We will use a hard-coded array instead of reading from a file. These values represent the values from the previous table, exclusive of the totals:

```
var matrix = [
    [11975, 5871, 8916, 2868],
    [1951, 10048, 2060, 6171],
    [8010, 16145, 8090, 8045],
    [1013, 990, 940, 6907]
];
```

We then use the d3.layout.chord() function to create the layout object for this graph.

```
var layout = d3.layout.chord()
    .padding(.05)
    .matrix(matrix);
```

.padding(0.05) states that there will be 0.05 radians of space between the sections on the outside of the diagram, and the call to .matrix() specifies the data to use.

The following line of code creates the colors that will be utilized (black, blondish, brownish, and reddish):

```
var fill = d3.scale.ordinal().domain(d3.range(4))
    .range(['#000000', '#FFEE89', '#957244', '#FF0023']);
```

Then, the ring segments are rendered. The inner and outer radius of the ring segments is calculated as percentages of the smallest dimension of the visual. The data that is bound is the group's property of the layout object. For each of these, we render a path using an arc generator:

```
var innerRadius = Math.min(width, height) * 0.41,
    outerRadius = innerRadius * 1.1;
mainGroup.append('g')
    .selectAll('path')
    .data(layout.groups)
    .enter()
    .append('path')
    .style('fill', function(d) { return fill(d.index); })
    .style('stroke', function(d) { return fill(d.index); })
    .attr('d', d3.svg.arc()
        .innerRadius(innerRadius)
        .outerRadius(outerRadius));
```

Next, the chords are rendered. A d3.svg.chord() function will be applied to each datum, and a path of the size innerRadius is generated:

```
mainGroup.append('g')
    .selectAll('path')
    .data(layout.chords)
    .enter()
    .append('path')
    .attr('d', d3.svg.chord()
              .radius(innerRadius))
    .style('fill', function(d) { return fill(d.target.index); })
    .style({
        opacity: 1,
        stroke: '#000',
        'fill-opacity': 0.67,
        'stroke-width': '0.5px'
    });
```

At this point, we have created the entire chord graph sans ticks and labels. We will omit covering those in the book, but feel free to check out the sample code with the text to see how this is performed.

Techniques to demonstrate the flow of information

The last two layouts and corresponding visualizations that we will examine help the viewer to understand how data changes as it flows over time or through intermediate points.

Using streamgraphs to show changes in values

A **streamgraph** demonstrates the change in values in a multiple series of data as a flowing stream of data. The height of each stream represents the value of that stream at that moment in time.

They are useful for demonstrating where certain categories start or stop at different points along the graph. Common examples are data such as box-office receipts or the number of listeners for various artists on streaming media as they change over time.

To demonstrate a streamgraph, we will use the data available at `https://goo.gl/HTL4HG`.

This data consists of four series of data:

```
[
  [ 20, 49, 67, 16,  0, 19, 19, 0,  0, 1, 10,  5, 6,  1,  1 ],
  [ 4,   6,  3, 34,  0, 16,  1, 2,  1, 1,  6,  0, 1, 56,  0 ],
  [ 2,   8, 13, 15,  0, 12, 23, 15,10, 1,  0,  1, 0,  0,  6 ],
  [ 3,   9, 28,  0, 91,  6,  1, 0,  0, 0,  7, 18, 0,  9, 16 ]
]
```

The online example is available at the following location:

bl.ock (10.8): `http://goo.gl/LMd3F3`

The following is the resulting streamgraph:

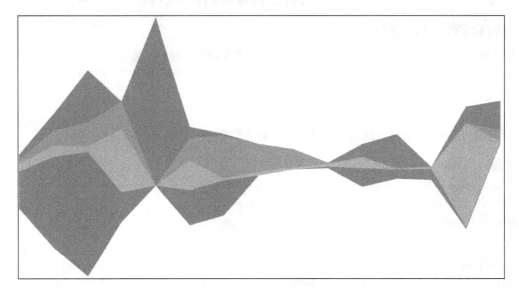

This graph allows us to see how each individual series of data is related to each other at each point of measurement. It is, in a way, like a stacked area chart, but instead of each being fixed at a common baseline, the bottom of the graph is also allowed to vary in location.

The example begins by loading the data and setting up the main SVG element:

```
var url = 'https://gist.githubusercontent.com/
d3byex/25129228aa50c30ef01f/raw/4393a0e579cbfd9bb20a431ce93c72fb1
ea23537/streamgraph.json';
d3.json(url, function (error, rawData) {
    var width = 960, height = 500;
    var svg = d3.select('body')
        .append('svg')
        .attr({
            'width': width,
            'height': height
        });
```

We need to massage the data a little bit, as the call to the layout function will expect it in the same format as an area graph, which is an array of arrays of objects with x and y properties. The following code creates this, using the position of the value in each array as the x value:

```
var data = Array();
d3.map(rawData, function (d, i) {
    data[i] = d.map(function (i, j) {
        return { x: j, y: i };
    });
});
```

Next, the code creates the axes, with the X axis being a linear axis representing the number of points in each series:

```
var numPointsPerLayer = data[0].length;

var xScale = d3.scale.linear()
    .domain([0, numPointsPerLayer - 1])
    .range([0, width]);
```

The layout is the familiar stack layout that was used in the area graph example, but we chain a call to `.offset('wiggle')`:

```
var layers = d3.layout.stack()
    .offset('wiggle')(data);
```

The remainder of the code continues just as an area graph, using an area path generator and similarly scaled Y axis.

Representing flows through multiple nodes

Instead of showing a continuous flow like a streamgraph, a **Sankey** diagram emphasizes how the flow quantity changes proportionally. This is somewhat like a chord diagram, but a Sankey has the ability to visualize more complex flows than just between two items.

In a Sankey diagram, the width of the lines between the nodes represents the volume of the flow between two nodes. Normally, flows start at one or more nodes on the left, flow through intermediates, and then terminate at nodes on the right.

The example diagram uses the data available at `https://goo.gl/1gQZBz`. This data consists of declarations for eight nodes and then the links between the nodes along with the amount of the flow between the nodes:

```json
{
"nodes":[
   {"node":0, "name":"Source 1"},
   {"node":1, "name":"Source 2"},
   {"node":2, "name":"First Level Distribution"},
   {"node":3, "name":"Second Level Distribution 1"},
   {"node":4, "name":"Terminus 1"},
   {"node":5, "name":"Terminus 2"},
   {"node":6, "name":"Second Level Distribution 2"},
   {"node":7, "name":"Source 3"}
],
"links":[
   {"source":0, "target":2, "value":6},
   {"source":0, "target":4, "value":2},

   {"source":1, "target":2, "value":4},
   {"source":1, "target":3, "value":2},
   {"source":1, "target":6, "value":1},

   {"source":2, "target":3, "value":5},
   {"source":2, "target":4, "value":3},
   {"source":2, "target":6, "value":2},

   {"source":3, "target":4, "value":4},
   {"source":3, "target":5, "value":4},

   {"source":6, "target":5, "value":5},
   {"source":7, "target":6, "value":2},
   {"source":7, "target":3, "value":1}
]
}
```

The online example is available at the following location:

 bl.ock (10.9): `http://goo.gl/exZkI4`

The resulting Sankey diagram from this data will be the following:

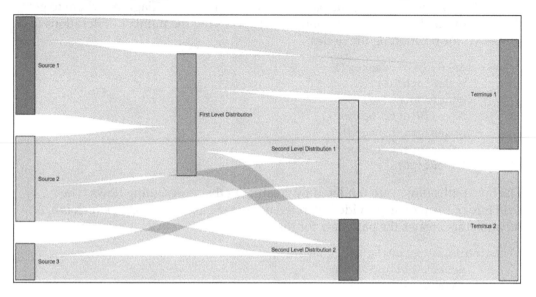

The Sankey layout is considered a plugin to D3.js. It is not in the base library, so you need to retrieve the code, and make sure to reference it in your app. This code is available at `https://github.com/d3/d3-plugins/tree/master/sankey`, or you can grab it from the book's example.

The example begins by loading the data and creating the main SVG elements:

```
var url = 'https://gist.githubusercontent.
com/d3byex/25129228aa50c30ef01f/raw/
e6ea7c4728e45fb8d0464b21686eec806687e117/sankey.json';
d3.json(url, function(error, graph) {
    var width = 950, height = 500;
    var svg = d3.select('body')
        .append('svg')
        .attr({
            width: width,
            height: height
        });
    var mainGroup = svg.append('g');
```

We create the layout using the plugin as follows. There are lot of parameters here to specify the size of the nodes, the padding, overall size of the diagram, where to get the links and nodes in your data, and layout specifying the number of iterations to be processed for positioning the nodes:

```
var sankey = d3.sankey()
    .nodeWidth(36)
    .nodePadding(40)
    .size([width, height])
    .nodes(graph.nodes)
    .links(graph.links)
    .layout(10);
```

The flow paths (links) are rendered by creating paths representing flows. The structure of the path is provided by referencing the `sankey.link()`, which is a function that creates the path data for the flow:

```
mainGroup.append('g')
    .selectAll('g.link')
    .data(data.links)
    .enter()
    .append('path')
    .attr({
        d: sankey.link(),
        fill: 'none',
        stroke: '#000',
        'stroke-opacity': 0.2,
        'stroke-width': function(d) { return Math.max(1, d.dy) }
    })
    .sort(function(a, b) { return b.dy - a.dy; });
```

Now we create a group to hold the nodes and place them into position based on the x and y properties provided by the layout. The `.node` style is used simply to differentiate the selection of these groups from those of the paths (which used `.link`):

```
var nodes = mainGroup.append('g')
    .selectAll('g.node')
    .data(data.nodes)
    .enter()
    .append('g')
    .attr('transform', function(d) {
        return 'translate(' + d.x + ',' + d.y + ')';
    });
```

Then, we insert a colored rectangle into the groups:

```
var color = d3.scale.category20();
nodes.append('rect')
    .attr({
        height: function(d) { return d.dy; },
        width: sankey.nodeWidth(),
        fill: function(d, i) {
            return d.color = color(i);
        },
        stroke: 'black'
    });
```

We also include text to describe the node, with some logic to position the label:

```
nodes.append('text')
    .attr({
        x: -6,
        y: function(d) { return d.dy / 2; },
        dy: '.35em',
        'text-anchor': 'end'
    })
    .style('font', '10px sans-serif')
    .text(function(d) { return d.name; })
    .filter(function(d) { return d.x < width / 2; })
    .attr({
        x: 6 + sankey.nodeWidth(),
        'text-anchor': 'start'
    });
```

Summary

We have covered a lot in this chapter. The overall focus was on creating complex graphs that utilize D3.js layout objects. These included a multitude of graphs in different categories including stacked, packed, clustered, flow-based, hierarchical, and radial.

One of the beauties of D3.js is the ease at which it allows you to create these complex visuals. They are pattern-oriented such that the code for each is often very similar, with just a slight change of layout objects.

In the next chapter, we will look at a specific type of graph in detail: the network diagram. These extend upon several concepts we have seen in this chapter, such as flow and hierarchy, to allow us to visualize very complex network data such as those found in social networks.

11
Visualizing Information Networks

In this chapter, we will examine a specific type of layout known as a **force-directed graph**. These are a type of visualization that are generally utilized to display network information: interconnected nodes.

A particularly common type of network visualization is of the relationships within a social network. A visualization of a social network can help you understand how different people have formed various relationships. These include links between others as well as the way groups of people form clusters or cliques of friends and how those groups interrelate.

D3.js provides extensive capabilities for creating very complex network visualizations using force-directed networks. We will overview a number of representative examples of these graphs, cover a little bit of the theory of how they operate, and dive into a few examples to demonstrate their creation and usage.

Specifically, in this chapter we will cover the following topics:

- A brief overview of force-directed graphs
- Creating a basic force-directed graph
- Modifying the length of the links
- Forcing nodes to move away from each other
- Labeling the nodes
- Forcing nodes to stay in place
- Expressing directionality and type with link visuals

An overview of force-directed graphs

There are a number of means of rendering network data. A particularly common one, which we will examine in this chapter, is to use a class of algorithms known as force-directed layouts.

These algorithms position the nodes in the graph in a two or three dimensional space. The positioning is performed by assigning forces along edges and nodes, and then these forces are used to simulate moving the nodes into a position where the amount of energy in the entire system is minimized.

The following is a representative picture of a force-directed graph from a Wiki. Nodes are pages, and the lines between the nodes represent the links between the pages. Node size varies based on the number of links in/out of a particular node:

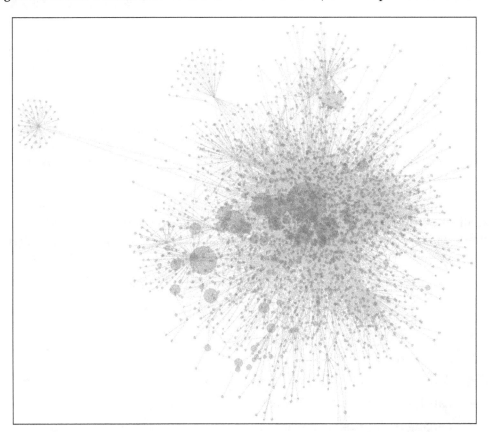

The fundamental components of a force-directed graph are the nodes in the graph and the relations between those nodes. The graph is iteratively laid out, usually animated during the process, and can take quite a few iterations to **stabilize**.

The force layout algorithm in D3.js takes into account a number of factors. A few of the important parameters of the algorithm and how they influence the simulation are the following:

- **Size (width and height)**: This represents an overall size of the diagram, and a center of gravity, normally the center of the diagram. Nodes in the diagram will tend to move towards this point. If nodes do not have an initial x and y position, then they will be placed randomly in a position between 0 and width in the x direction and height in the y direction.

- **Charge**: This describes how much a node attracts other nodes. Negative values push away other nodes, and positive numbers attract. The larger the value in either direction, the stronger is the force in that direction.

- **Charge distance**: This specifies the maximum distance over which charge has effect (it defaults to infinity). Smaller values assist in performance of the layout, and result in a more localized layout of nodes in clusters.

- **Friction**: Represents an amount of velocity delay. This value should be in the range of [0, 1]. At each tick of the layout, the velocity of every node is multiplied by this value. Using a value of 0 therefore, freezes all nodes in place, and 1 is a frictionless environment. Values in between eventually slow the nodes to a point where overall motion is small enough, and the simulation can be considered complete as the total amount of movement falls below the layout threshold at which point the graph is referred to as stable.

- **Link distance**: This specifies a desired distance between nodes at the end of the simulation. At each tick of the simulation, the distance between linked nodes is compared to this value, and nodes move towards or away from each other to try to reach the desired distance.

- **Link strength**: This is a value in the range of [0, 1], specifying how stretchable the link distance is during the simulation. A value of 0 is rigid and 1 is completely flexible.

- **Gravity**: This specifies an attraction of each node to the center of the layout. This is a weak geometric constraint. That is, the higher the overall gravity, the further away it is from the center of the rendering. This value is useful for keeping layouts relatively centered in the diagram and in keeping disconnected nodes from flying out to infinity.

We will go over enough of these parameters to get a good feel for making useful visualizations.

More detail on all the layout parameters is available at `https://github.com/mbostock/d3/wiki/Force-Layout`.

In addition to the parameters that facilitate the actual layout of the nodes, it is also possible to use other visual in a force-directed graph to convey various values in the underlying information:

- The color of a node can be used to distinguish nodes of particular types, such as people versus employers, or by their relation, such as all persons who work at a particular employer, or how many degrees of separation the node is from another node.

- The size of a node, which generally represents the magnitude of importance of the node. Often the number of links influence the size of a node.

- The thickness of the rendering of a link can be used to demonstrate that certain links have more influence than others or that the links are of particular types, that is, highways versus railways.

- The directionality of link, showing that the link has either no directionality or is one or bi-directional.

A simple force-directed graph

Our first example will demonstrate how to construct a force-directed graph. The online example is available at the following link:

 bl.ock (11.1): `http://goo.gl/ZyxCej`

All our force-directed graphs will start by loading data that represents a network. This example uses the data at `https://gist.githubusercontent.com/d3byex/5a8267f90a0d215fcb3e/raw/ba3b2e3065ca8eafb375f01155dc99c569fae66b/uni_network.json`.

The following are the contents of the file at the preceding link:

```
{
    "nodes": [
        { "name": "Mike" },
        { "name": "Marcia" },
        { "name": "Chrissy" },
        { "name": "Selena" },
        { "name": "William" },
        { "name": "Mikael" },
        { "name": "Bleu" },
        { "name": "Tagg" },
        { "name": "Bob" },
        { "name": "Mona" }
    ],
    "edges": [
        { "source": 0, "target": 1 },
        { "source": 0, "target": 4 },
        { "source": 0, "target": 5 },
        { "source": 0, "target": 6 },
        { "source": 0, "target": 7 },
        { "source": 1, "target": 2 },
        { "source": 1, "target": 3 },
        { "source": 1, "target": 5 },
        { "source": 1, "target": 8 },
        { "source": 1, "target": 9 },
    ]
}
```

The force-directed layout algorithms in D3.js require the data to be in this format. This needs to be an object with a nodes and an edges property. The nodes property can be an array of any other objects you like to use. These are typically your data items.

The edges array must consist of objects with both source and target properties, and the value for each is the index into the nodes array of the source and target nodes. You can add other properties, but we need to supply at least these two.

To start rendering the graph, we load this data and get the main SVG element created:

```
var url = 'https://gist.githubusercontent.
com/d3byex/5a8267f90a0d215fcb3e/raw/
ba3b2e3065ca8eafb375f01155dc99c569fae66b/uni_network.json';
d3.json(url, function(error, data) {
    var width = 960, height = 500;
    var svg = d3.select('body').append('svg')
        .attr({
            width: width,
            height: height
        });
```

The next step is to create the layout for the graph using `d3.layout.force()`. There are many options, several of which we will explore over the course of our examples, but we start with the following:

```
var force = d3.layout.force()
    .nodes(data.nodes)
    .links(data.edges)
    .size([width, height])
    .start();
```

This informs the layout about the location of the nodes and links using the `.node()` and `.link()` functions respectively. The call to `.size()` informs the layout about the area to constrain the layout within and has two effects on the graph: the gravitational center and the initial random position.

The call to `.start()` begins the simulation, and must be called after the layout is created and the nodes and links are assigned. If the nodes and links change later, it can be called again to restart the simulation. Note that the simulation starts after this function returns, not immediately. So, you can still make other changes to the visual.

Now we can render the links and nodes:

```
var edges = svg.selectAll('line')
    .data(data.edges)
    .enter()
    .append('line')
    .style('stroke', '#ccc')
    .style('stroke-width', 1);
```

```
var colors = d3.scale.category20();
var nodes = svg
    .selectAll('circle')
    .data(data.nodes)
    .enter()
    .append('circle')
    .attr('r', 10)
    .attr('fill', function(d, i) {
        return colors(i);
    })
    .call(force.drag);
```

Note that we also chained the .call() function passing it a reference to the force. drag function of our layout. This function is provided by the layout object to easily allow us a means of dragging the nodes in the network.

There is one more step required. A force layout is a simulation and consists of a sequence of **ticks** that we must handle. Each tick represents that the layout algorithm has passed over the nodes and recalculated their positions, and this gives us the opportunity to reposition the visuals.

To hook into the ticks, we can use the force.on() function, telling it that we want to listen to tick events, and on each event, call a function to allow us to reposition our visuals. The following is our function for this activity:

```
force.on('tick', function() {
    edges.attr({
        x1: function(d) { return d.source.x; },
        y1: function(d) { return d.source.y; },
        x2: function(d) { return d.target.x; },
        y2: function(d) { return d.target.y; }
    });

    nodes.attr('cx', function(d) { return d.x; })
        .attr('cy', function(d) { return d.y; });
});
```

On each tick, we need to reposition each node and edge appropriately. Notice how we are doing this. D3.js has added to our data x and a y properties, which are the calculated position. It also has added a px and py property to each data node, which represents the previous x and y position.

You can also use start and end as parameters of the on() method to trap when the simulation begins and completes.

On running this, the output will be similar to the following:

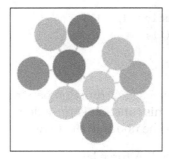

Every time this example is executed, the nodes will finish in a different position. This is due to the algorithm specifying a random start position for each node.

The nodes are very close in this example, to the point where the links are almost not visible. But it is possible to drag the nodes with the mouse, which will expose the links. Also notice that the layout is executed while you drag and the nodes snap back to the middle when the dragged node is released.

Using link distance to spread out the nodes

These nodes in the previous example are a little too close together and we have a hard time seeing the edges. To add more distance between the nodes, we can specify a link distance. This is demonstrated by the following example:

 bl.ock (11.2): http://goo.gl/dd1T30

The one modification this example makes to the previous one is that it increases the link distance to 200 (the default is 20):

```
var force = d3.layout.force()
    .nodes(data.nodes)
    .links(data.edges)
    .size([width, height])
    .linkDistance(200)
    .start();
```

This modification results in some better spacing of the nodes at the end of the simulation:

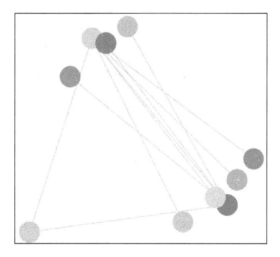

Drag the nodes around. It will demonstrate some of the physics in play:

- No matter where you move any node(s), the graph returns to the center of the visualization. This is the effect of gravity on the layout and of it being placed in the center.

- The nodes always come together, but are always at least the link distance apart. The gravity attracts them to the center and the default charge, which is -30, makes the nodes push away from each other, but not enough to stretch the links much or make the nodes escape the center of gravity.

- The preceding point has an important ramification in the result of the visualization. The links between nodes will generally cross each other. In many network visualizations, it is desirable to try and make the links not cross each other, as it simplifies the ability to follow the links, and hence, the relationships. We will examine how to fix this in the next example.

Adding repulsion to nodes for preventing crossed links

The means by which we attempt to prevent crossing links is to apply an amount of repulsion to each of the nodes. When the amount of repulsion exceeds the pull of the center of gravity, the nodes can move away from this point. They will also move away from the other nodes, tending to expand the result graph out to a maximum size, with the effect of causing the links to not cross.

The following example demonstrates node repulsion:

 bl.ock (11.3): `http://goo.gl/PCHK68`

This example makes two modifications to the previous example:

```
var force = d3.layout.force()
    .nodes(data.nodes)
    .links(data.edges)
    .size([width, height])
    .linkDistance(1)
    .charge(-5000)
    .start();
```

This creates a charge with a value of -5000, meaning that the nodes actually repulse each other. There is also a smaller link distance, as the repulsion will push the nodes apart quite a bit, therefore stretching the links. Leaving the links at 200 would make the links very long.

When this simulation completes, you will have a graph that looks like the following:

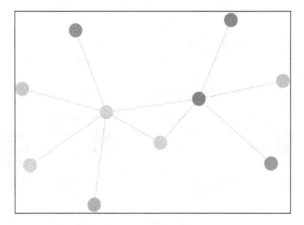

Notice how the nodes now tried to get as far away from each other as possible! The links were stretched quite a bit too, event though the link distance is set to 1. Links are, by default, elastic and will be stretched or compressed based on the charges and gravity in the system.

Rerun this simulation again and again. You will notice that it almost always converges to this same shape with the nodes in the same relative places in the graph (the group itself will likely be rotated a different amount each time). In a really rare case, there may still be a crossed edge, but the repulsion is set high enough to prevent this for most executions.

Labelling the nodes

Something that has been missing in our force-directed graphs is labelling of the nodes so that we can tell what data the nodes represent. The following example demonstrates how to add labels to the nodes:

bl.ock (11.4): `http://goo.gl/31VfSU`

The difference in this preceding example is that instead of representing a node by a single circle SVG element, we represent it by a group which contains both a circle and a text element:

```
var nodes = svg.selectAll('g')
    .data(data.nodes)
    .enter()
    .append('g')
    .call(force.drag);

var colors = d3.scale.category20();
nodes.append('circle')
    .attr('r', 10)
    .attr('fill', function (d, i) {
        return colors(i);
    })
    .call(force.drag);

nodes.append('text')
    .attr({
            dx: 12,
            dy: '.35em',
```

```
                    'pointer-events': 'none'
        })
    .style('font', '10px sans-serif')
    .text(function (d) { return d.name });
```

Then we need one more change during the processing of the tick event. Since we now need to position an SVG group instead of a circle, this code needs to translate the group into position instead of using the x and y properties:

```
force.on('tick', function () {
    edges.each(function (d) {
        d3.select(this).attr({
            x1: d.source.x,
            y1: d.source.y,
            x2: d.target.x,
            y2: d.target.y
        });
    });

    nodes.attr('transform', function (d) {
    return 'translate(' + d.x + ',' + d.y + ')';
    });
});
```

The result of this example now looks like the following:

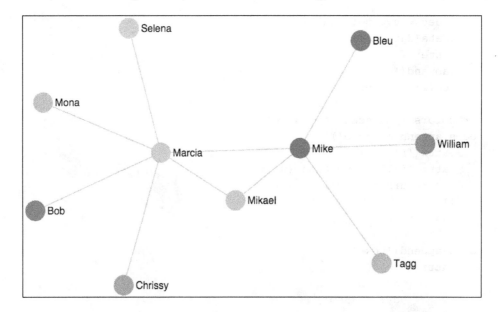

Making nodes stick in place

A common—and frustrating—issue when examining nodes in a force network is that when you move one node of a clump of other nodes to see it better and then let it go, it goes back to where it was. I'll bet you've experienced this madness already just while using these examples.

The can be remidied by using a concept known as making the nodes sticky. The following example demonstrates this in operation:

bl.ock (11.5): `http://goo.gl/nmQu3d`

Now, when you drag a node, it will stay where you leave it. Nodes that are fixed in place will change to have a thick black border. To release a node, double click it and it will be put back into the force layout.

The following image shows this with three nodes fixed in place:

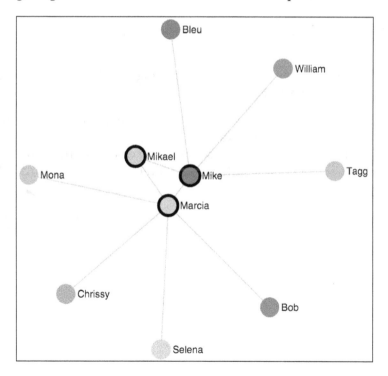

Now let's examine the modifications needed to make this work. This works by adding a few function chains to our code to create the circles:

```
nodes.append('circle')
    .attr('r', 10)
    .attr({
        r: 10,
        fill: function(d, i) {
            return colors(i);
        },
        stroke: 'black',
        'stroke-width': 0
    })
    .call(force.drag()
        .on("dragstart", function(d) {
            d.fixed = true;
            d3.select(this).attr('stroke-width', 3);
        }))
    .on('dblclick', function(d) {
        d.fixed = false;
        d3.select(this).attr('stroke-width', 0);
    });
```

When the circle is first created, in addition to having its fill color specified, it will also have a stroke color of black but of width 0.

Then, instead of using .call(force.drag), we replace that with a custom drag implementation. At the start of the drag, the code sets a property, fixed, on the data object to true. If the force layout object sees that the object has this property, and its value is true, then it will not attempt to reposition the item. And then, the border is set to be three pixels in width.

The last modification is to handle the dblclick mouse event, which will set the fixed property to false, releasing the node to be part of the layout and then hiding the thick border.

Adding directionality markers and style to the links

Relationships between a node can be one-way or bi-directional. The code we have written so far assumed one-way, or perhaps, non-directional. Let's now look at how we can express the direction in the relationship by adding arrow heads to the lines.

The example we will create will assume that each entry in the edges collection of the data represents a one-way link from the source to the target. If there is a bi-directional link, there will be an additional entry in edges with the source and target reversed.

The example will use the data from `https://gist.githubusercontent.com/ d3byex/5a8267f90a0d215fcb3e/raw/8469d2a7da14c1c8180ebb2ea8ddf1e2944f9 90c/multi_network.html`, which has several bi-directional links added as well as a `type` property to specify the type of the relationship.

The edges collection in this data is the following. The nodes have not changed:

```
"edges": [
    { "source": 0, "target":  1, "type": "spouse" },
    { "source": 1, "target":  0, "type": "spouse" },
    { "source": 0, "target":  4, "type": "coworker"},
    { "source": 4, "target":  0, "type": "coworker"},
    { "source": 0, "target":  5, "type": "father" },
    { "source": 5, "target":  0, "type": "son" },
    { "source": 0, "target":  6, "type": "master" },
    { "source": 6, "target":  0, "type": "pet" },
    { "source": 0, "target":  7, "type": "master" },
    { "source": 1, "target":  2, "type": "spouse" },
    { "source": 1, "target":  3, "type": "friend" },
    { "source": 1, "target":  5, "type": "mother" },
    { "source": 1, "target":  8, "type": "pet" },
    { "source": 8, "target":  1, "type": "master" },
    { "source": 1, "target":  9, "type": "pet" },
    { "source": 5, "target": 10, "type": "pet" }
]
```

bl.ock (11.6): `https://goo.gl/hucTe1`

The following image depicts the result of this example:

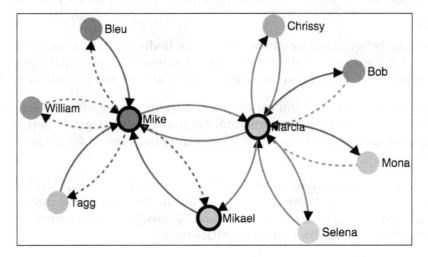

Let's see how the code goes about creating this visualization.

The first thing that is changed in this example is that it uses styles to color the different types of links:

```
.link {
    fill: none;
    stroke: #666;
    stroke-width: 1.5px;
}

.link.spouse {
    stroke: green;
}

.link.son {
    stroke: blue;
}

.link.father {
    stroke: blue;
    stroke-dasharray: 0, 2, 1;
}

.link.friend {
```

```
    stroke: teal;
}

.link.pet {
    stroke: purple;
}

.link.master {
    stroke: purple;
    stroke-dasharray: 0, 2, 1;
}

.link.ruler {
    stroke: red;
    stroke-dasharray: 0, 2, 1;
}

.link.coworker {
    stroke: green;
    stroke-dasharray: 0, 2, 1;
}
```

The code to load the data and to set up the SVG element and the force layout is the same as the last example. The other difference is that the code needs to determine the specifc link types as they will be used for markers and styles:

```
var linkTypes = d3.set(data.edges.map(function (d) {
    return d.type;
})).values();
```

Next, there are markers created for each of the link types. These will render a curved path with an arrow head on each end, created by the last chained function to set the d attribute:

```
svg.append("defs")
    .selectAll("marker")
    .data(linkTypes)
    .enter()
    .append("marker")
    .attr({
        id: function (d) { return d; },
        viewBox: "0 -5 10 10",
        refX: 15,
```

```
            refY: -1.5,
            markerWidth: 6,
            markerHeight: 6,
            orient: "auto"
    })
    .append("path")
    .attr("d", "M0,-5L10,0L0,5");
```

The next step is to create the edges:

```
var edges = svg.append("g")
    .selectAll("path")
    .data(force.links())
    .enter()
    .append("path")
    .attr("class", function (d) {
        return "link " + d.type;
    })
    .attr("marker-end", function(d) {
        return "url(#" + d.type + ")";
    });
```

Instead of using a line, the code now uses a path. The d property of the path is not specified at this time. It will be set at every tick of the simulation. This path references one of the styles by using the type as part of the class name, and the marker-end attributes specifies which marker definition to use for this segment.

The circles are created in the same manner as the previous example, and so is the text. The last change is that the tick handler is modified to not only reposition the nodes, but to also regenerate paths based on arcs:

```
force.on("tick", function () {
    edges.attr("d", function (d) {
        var dx = d.target.x - d.source.x,
            dy = d.target.y - d.source.y,
            dr = Math.sqrt(dx * dx + dy * dy);
        return "M" + d.source.x + "," + d.source.y + "A" +
                dr + "," + dr + " 0 0,1 " +
                d.target.x + "," + d.target.y;
    });
    nodes.attr("transform", function (d) {
        return "translate(" + d.x + "," + d.y + ")";
    });
});
```

Summary

In this chapter, we explained how to use D3.js for generating force-directed graphs. These types of graphs are some of the most interesting types of graphs and can be used to visualize large sets of interconnected data such as social networks.

The chapter started by going over the basic concepts of creating a graph, stepping through an example that progressively refined the graph, while making the effort to demonstrate how several of the parameters effect the result of the graph.

We then covered several techniques for enhancing and making the graphs more usable. These included labeling nodes with text, replacing nodes with images, and styling links to show direction and type.

In the next chapter, we will cover using D3.js for creating maps. We will also learn quite a bit about GeoJSON and TopoJSON, both of which, when combined with D3.js, allow us to create complex visuals based on geographic data.

12
Creating Maps with GeoJSON and TopoJSON

D3.js provides extensive capabilities for creating maps and to facilitate you in presenting data as part of the map or as an overlay. The functions for mapping within D3.js leverage a data format known as GeoJSON, a form of JSON that encodes geographic information.

Another common type of data for maps in D3.js is TopoJSON. TopoJSON is a more compressed form of GeoJSON. Both these formats are used to represent the cartographic information required to create a map, and D3.js processes this data and performs its usual magic of converting this information into SVG paths that visualize the map.

This chapter wills start with a brief overview of GeoJSON and TopoJSON. This will give you the foundation to understand how maps are represented and rendered with D3.js. We will then jump into many examples using both data formats for rendering maps of various types, coloring the geometries within the map based upon data, and for overlaying information at specific locations on those maps.

The specific topics that we will cover in this chapter include:

- A brief overview of TopoJSON and GeoJSON
- Drawing a map of the United States with GeoJSON
- Using TopoJSON to draw the countries of the world
- Styling the geometries that comprise a map
- Panning and zooming of a map

- Interaction with a globe
- Highlighting the boundaries of geometries on `mouseover` events
- Adding symbols to a map at specific locations
- Rendering maps of regions based upon data (using a choropleth)

Introducing TopoJSON and GeoJSON

Almost every map example in D3.js will use either **GeoJSON** or **TopoJSON**. GeoJSON is an open, standard, JSON-based format for representing basic geographical features as well as the non-spatial properties for those features (such as the name of a city or a landmark).

The core geometries in GeoJSON are points, line strings, and polygons. The basic description of a GeoJSON entity uses the following syntax:

```
{
    "type": name of the type of geometry (point, line string, ...)
    "coordinates": one or more tuple of latitude / longitude
}
```

Let's take a look at the four basic types of geometry types available in GeoJSON. A **point** represents a position in two-dimensional space, and consists of a pair of one latitude and longitude. A point is normally used to specify the location of a feature on a map (such as a building):

Example	Representative GeoJSON
	```{ "type": "Point", "coordinates": [30, 10] }```

`LineString` describes a sequence of points which have a line drawn between them, starting at the first, through all intermediate points, and ending at the last coordinate. The name conjures up visions of stretching a string caught between all the points. These shapes are normally used to represent items such as, roads or rivers:

Example	Representative GeoJSON
	```{ "type": "LineString", "coordinates": [[30, 10], [10, 30], [40, 40]] }```

A **polygon** is a closed shape normally consisting of three or more points, where the last point is the same as the first and forms a closed shape. The JSON representation is shown as follows; note that the coordinates are an array of arrays of tuples:

Example	Representative GeoJSON
	```{ "type": "Polygon", "coordinates": [[[30, 10], [40, 40], [20, 40], [10, 20], [30, 10]]] }```

The purpose of an array of arrays of tuples is to allow multiple polygons to be defined, which exclude each other, thereby allowing the exclusions of one or more polygonal regions within one another:

Example	Representative GeoJSON
	```{ "type": "Polygon", "coordinates": [[[35, 10], [45, 45], [15, 40], [10, 20], [35, 10]], [[20, 30], [35, 35], [30, 20], [20, 30]]] }```

It is possible to define multi-part geometries where a particular geometry type is reused, and where the coordinates describe multiple instances of the type of geometry. These types are the previous types prefaced with *Multi*—`MultiPoint`, `MultiLineString`, and `MultiPolygon`. Each is demonstrated as follows:

Type	Example	Representative GeoJSON
MultiPoint		```{ "type": "MultiPoint", "coordinates": [[10, 40], [40, 30], [20, 20], [30, 10]] }```
MultiLineString		```{ "type": MultiLineString", "coordinates": [[[10, 10], [20, 20], [10, 40]], [[40, 40], [30, 30], [40, 20], [30, 10]]] }```
MultiPolygon		```{ "type": "MultiPolygon", "coordinates": [[[[40, 40], [20, 45], [45, 30], [40, 40]]], [[[20, 35], [10, 30], [10, 10], [30, 5], [45, 20], [20, 35]], [[30, 20], [20, 15], [20, 25], [30, 20]]]] }```

These basic geometries can be wrapped within a **feature**. A feature contains a geometry and also a set of properties. As an example, the following defines a feature which consists of a point geometry, and which has a single property, name, which can be used to describe a name for that feature:

```
{
    "type": "Feature",
    "geometry": {
      "type": "Point",
      "coordinates": [46.862633, -114.011593]
    },
    "properties": {
      "name": "Missoula"
    }
}
```

We can go up one more level in the hierarchy, and define what is known as a **feature collection**:

```
{
      "type": "FeatureCollection",
      "features": [
        { "type": "Feature",
          "geometry": {"type": "Point",
          "coordinates": [102.0, 0.5]},
          "properties": {"prop0": "value0"} },
        { "type": "Feature",
          "geometry": {
            "type": "LineString",
            "coordinates": [
              [102.0, 0.0], [103.0, 1.0],[104.0, 0.0], [105.0, 1.0]]
            },
          "properties": { "prop0": "value0", "prop1": 0.0 }
          },
        { "type": "Feature",
          "geometry": {
            "type": "Polygon",
            "coordinates": [
              [ [100.0, 0.0], [101.0, 0.0], [101.0, 1.0],
                [100.0, 1.0], [100.0, 0.0] ]   ]
          },
          "properties": {
            "prop0": "value0", "prop1": {"this": "that"} }
          }
        ]
      }
```

By combining geometries, features, and feature collections, it is possible to describe very complex shapes such as maps.

But one of the problems with GeoJSON is that it is very verbose, and particular geometries and features cannot be reused. If the same geometry is required in multiple locations, it must be completely specified a second time.

To help fix this situation, TopoJSON was created. TopoJSON provides additional constructs for the encoding of topology and reuse. Instead of discretely describing each geometry, TopoJSON allows you to define geometries, and then stitch them together using concepts known as **arcs**.

Arcs allows TopoJSON to eliminate redundancy, and to provide a much more compact representation as compared to GeoJSON. It is stated that TopoJSON can commonly provide 80 percent compression over GeoJSON. With every millisecond of the download time of a web page being important, this can be significant for user experience when using large sets of geometry.

A full explanation of TopoJSON is a bit beyond the scope of this book, but to briefly demonstrate it, we can look at the following and briefly examine its content:

```
{
  "type": "Topology",
  "objects": {
    "example": {
      "type": "GeometryCollection",
      "geometries": [
        { "type": "Point",
          "properties": {
            "prop0": "value0" },
          "coordinates": [102, 0.5]
        },
        { "type": "LineString",
          "properties": {
            "prop0": "value0",
            "prop1": 0 },
          "arcs": [0]
        },
        { "type": "Polygon",
          "properties": {
            "prop0": "value0",
            "prop1": {
              "this": "that"
            }
          },
```

```
            "arcs": [[-2]]
          }
        ]
      }
    },
    "arcs": [
      [[102, 0], [103, 1], [104, 0], [105, 1]],
      [[100, 0], [101, 0], [101, 1], [100, 1], [100, 0]]  ]
  }
```

This TopoJSON object has three properties: `type`, `objects`, and `arcs`. The value of `type` is always `"topology"`. The `objects` property consists of a geometry collection similar to those in GeoJSON, with the difference that instead of specifying coordinates, the object can, instead, specify one or more arcs.

Arcs are the big difference in TopoJSON versus GeoJSON, and represent the means of reuse. The arcs property provides an array of arrays of positions, where a position is essentially a coordinate.

These arcs are referenced by geometries of 0-based array semantics. Hence, the `LineString` geometry in the preceding code is referencing the first arc in the topology object by specifying `arcs[0]`.

The polygon object is referencing an arc with value `-2`. A negative arc value specifies that the one's complement of the arc that should be utilized. This essentially infers that the positions in the arc should be reversed. Therefore, `-2` instructs to get the reversed position of the second arc. This is one of the strategies that TopoJSON uses to reuse and compress data.

There are other options, such as transforms and bounding boxes, and other rules. For a more detailed specification, please see `https://github.com/mbostock/topojson-specification`.

An important thing to note about TopoJSON is that D3.js itself only uses GeoJSON data. To use data in the TopoJSON format, you will need to use the TopoJSON plugin available at `https://github.com/mbostock/topojson`. This plugin will convert TopoJSON into GeoJSON that can be used by D3.js functions, thereby affording the capabilities of TopoJSON to your D3.js application.

Creating a map of the United States

Our first examples will examine creating a map of the United States. We will start with an example that loads the data and gets the map rendered, and then we will examine styling the map to make it more visible, followed by examples of modifying the projection used to render the content more effectively.

Creating our first map of the United States with GeoJSON

Our first map will render the United States. We will use a GeoJSON data file, `us-states.json`, available at `https://gist.githubusercontent.com/d3byex/65a128a9a499f7f0b37d/raw/176771c2f08dbd3431009ae27bef9b2f2fb56e36/us-states.json`. The following are the first few lines of this file, and demonstrate how the shapes of the states are organized within the file:

```
{"type":"FeatureCollection","features":[
  { "type": "Feature",
    "id": "01",
    "properties": { "name": "Alabama" },
    "geometry": {
      "type": "Polygon",
      "coordinates": [ [
          [ -87.359296, 35.00118 ], [ -85.606675, 34.984749 ],
          [ -85.431413, 34.124869 ], [ -85.184951, 32.859696 ],
          [ -85.069935, 32.580372 ], [ -84.960397, 32.421541 ],
          [ -85.004212, 32.322956 ], [ -84.889196, 32.262709 ],
  . . .
```

`FeatureCollection` at the top level consists of an array of features, each element of which is a state (or territory) as well as Washington D.C. Each state is a feature, has a single property `Name`, and a polygon geometry representing the outline of the state expressed in latitude and longitude tuples.

The code for the example is available at the following link:

bl.ock (12.1): `http://goo.gl/dzKsVd`

On opening the URL, you will see the following map:

The code required to take this data and render a map is sublimely simple (by design). It begins by creating the main SVG element:

```
var width = 950, height = 500;
var svg = d3.select('body')
    .append('svg')
    .attr({
        width: width,
        height: height
    });
```

GeoJSON is simply JSON and can be loaded with d3.json():

```
var url = 'https://gist.githubusercontent.com/
d3byex/65a128a9a499f7f0b37d/raw/176771c2f08dbd3431009ae27bef9b2f2fb5
6e36/us-states.json';
d3.json(url, function (error, data) {
    var path = d3.geo.path();
    svg.selectAll('path')
        .data(data.features)
        .enter()
        .append('path')
        .attr('d', path);
});
d3.json("/data/us-states.json", function (error, data) {
```

Once we have the data, we can then create a `d3.geo.path()`. This object has the smarts for taking the features in the GeoJSON and converting them into an SVG path. The code then adds a path to the main SVG element, binds the data, and sets the `d` property of the path to our `d3.geo.path()` object.

Wow, with just a few lines of code, we have drawn a map of the United States!

Styling the map of the United States

Overall, this image is dark, and the borders between the states are not particularly visible. We can change this by providing a style for the fill and stroke values used to render the map.

The code for this example is available at the following link:

bl.ock (12.2): `https://goo.gl/chhKjz`

When opening this URL, you will see the following map:

The only change to the previous example is to set the fill to transparent, and the borders to black:

```
svg.selectAll('path')
   .data(data.features)
   .enter()
   .append('path')
   .attr('d', path)
      .style({ fill: 'none', stroke: 'black' });
```

Using the albersUsa projection

You may have a few questions about the map in the previous two examples. First, how is the map scaled to the size of the SVG element? Second, can I change this scale? And why are Alaska and Hawaii drawn down where Mexico would normally be?

These are related to some underlying assumptions about a **projection**. A projection is a way of taking geographic data, which is 2D data (latitude and longitude), but which is really on a three dimensional sphere (the earth), and rendering it onto a 2D surface with specific dimensions (your computer screen or viewport in the browser).

In this example, D3.js made some implicit assumptions on these factors. To help exemplify these assumptions, suppose we change the SVG element to be of size 500 x 250. When running this, we get the following output:

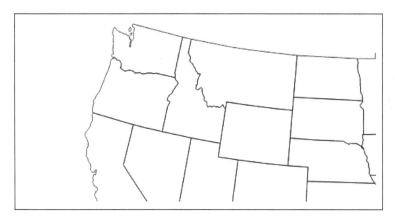

The code that creates this is available at the following location. The only change from the previous example is that the height and width of the SVG element have each been halved:

bl.ock (12.3): http://goo.gl/41wyCY

The result is that the actual rendering is the same size, and we have clipped the lower and rightmost three-quarters of the map due to the smaller container.

Why is this? It is because, by default, D3.js uses a projection known as an **albersUsa** projection, which has a number of assumptions that come with it:

- The dimensions of the resulting map are 1024 x 728
- The map is centered at half of the width and height (512, 364)
- The projection also places Alaska and Hawaii in the lower-left side of the map (aha!)

To change these assumptions, we can create our own albersUsa projection using a d3.geo.albersUsa() projection object. This object can be used to specify both a translation and scaling of the rendering of the results.

The following example creates an albersUsa projection and centers the map:

bl.ock (12.4): http://goo.gl/1e4DGp

With the following result:

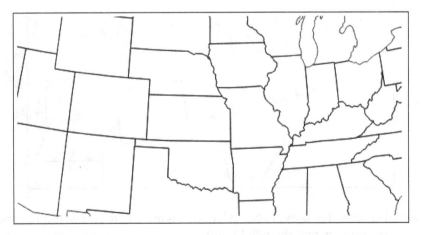

The code creates a d3.geo.albersUsa projection, and tells it to center the map of the United States at [width/2, height/2]:

```
var projection = d3.geo.albersUsa()
    .translate([width / 2, height / 2]);
```

The projection object then needs to be assigned to the d3.geo.path() object using its .projection() function:

```
var path = d3.geo.path()
    .projection(projection);
```

We have translated the center of the map, but the scale is still the same size. To change the scale, we use the projection's .scale() function. The following example sets the scale to the width, telling D3.js that the width of the map should not be 1024, but the value of width and height:

bl.ock (12.5): http://goo.gl/O51jPN

The preceding example results in a properly scaled map:

The only difference in the code is the call to .scale() on the projection:

```
var projection = d3.geo.albersUsa()
    .translate([width / 2, height / 2])
    .scale([width]);
```

Note that we only pass a single value to scale. The projection scales along the width, and then automatically and proportionately along the height.

Creating a flat map of the world

The **albersUsa** projection is one of many D3.js supplied projection objects. You can see the full list of these projections at `https://github.com/mbostock/d3/wiki/ Geo-Projections`.

We don't have space to demonstrate all of these in this book, but a few are worth the effort to demonstrate a couple of TopoJSON concepts. Specifically, we will demonstrate the rendering of a map of the countries of the world, sourced from TopoJSON, and projected onto both flat and spherical surfaces.

For data in these examples, will use the `world-110m.json` data file provided with the TopoJSON data library source code available at `https://gist. githubusercontent.com/d3byex/65a128a9a499f7f0b37d/raw/176771c2f08dbd3 431009ae27bef9b2f2fb56e36/world-110m.json`.

This data represents country data with features, specified at a 110-meter resolution.

Loading and rendering with TopoJSON

Now let's examine loading and rendering of TopoJSON. The following example demonstrates the process:

 bl.ock (12.6): `http://goo.gl/aLhKKe`

The code does not vary much from the previous example. The change comes after the data is loaded:

```
var path = d3.geo.path();
var countries = topojson.feature(world,
                         world.objects.countries).features;
svg.selectAll('path')
    .data(countries)
    .enter()
    .append('path')
    .attr('d', path)
    .style({
        fill: 'black',
        stroke: 'white'
    });
```

The example still uses a `d3.geo.path()` object, but this object cannot directly be given the TopoJSON. What needs to be done is to first extract the portion of this data that represents the countries, which is done by calling the `topojson.feature()` function.

The `topojson` variable is globally declared in the `topojson.js` file. Its `.feature()` function, when given a TopoJSON object (in this case, `world`), and a `GeometryCollection` (in this case, `world.objects.countries`), returns a GeoJSON feature that can be used by a path.

The selection to render the map then binds to this result, giving us the following map:

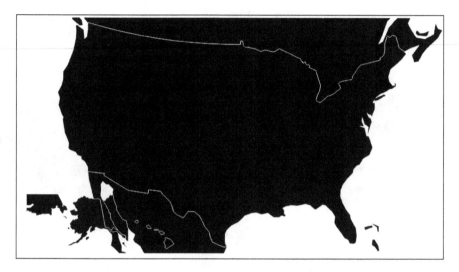

Whoops! That's not what we expected (but as we will see, it is exactly what we coded). Why is everything globed together? It is because we are still using the default projection, a `d3.geo.albersUsa()` projection.

Creating a map of the world using a Mercator projection

To fix this, we simply need to create a Mercator projection object, and apply it to the path. This is a well known projection that renders the map of the globe in a rectangular area.

The process is demosntrated in the following example:

bl.ock (12.7): `http://goo.gl/IWQPte`

The only difference in this code is the setup of the path to use a Mercator projection object:

```
var projection = d3.geo.mercator()
    .scale((width + 1) / 2 / Math.PI)
    .translate([width / 2, height / 2]);
var path = d3.geo.path().projection(projection);
```

We need to give the projection object a little information about the width and height of our rendering, and the resulting map is now the following, which looks a lot more like the familiar world map:

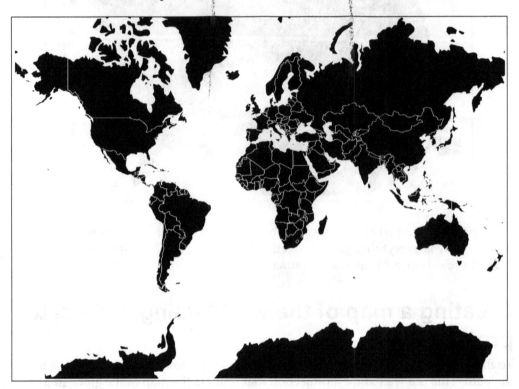

Creating spherical maps with orthographic projection

Now let's change our projection to an **orthographic** projection. This projection maps data on to a simulated sphere. This is demonstrated by the following example:

bl.ock (12.8): `http://goo.gl/M464W8`

This example simply changes the previous one by using a `d3.geo.orthographic()` projection object:

```
var projection = d3.geo.orthographic();
var path = d3.geo.path().projection(projection);
```

The preceding example code gives us this beautiful rendering of the planet:

If you examine this closely, you will notice that it is not quite perfect. Notice that Australia seems to be colliding with Africa and Madagascar, and New Zealand is seen in the South Atlantic ocean.

This is because this projection renders through all 360 degrees of the globe, and we are essentially seeing through a clear globe to the backside of the land masses on the far side.

To fix this, we can use the `.clipAngle()` function of the Mercator projection. The parameter is the number of degrees around the center point to which the landmasses should be rendered.

The following example demonstrates this in action:

 bl.ock (12.9): `http://goo.gl/G28ir0`

This changes one line of code:

```
var projection = d3.geo.orthographic()
    .clipAngle(90);
```

And gives us the following result:

It may not be apparent in the image provided in the book, but this image of the globe on the web page is fairly small. We can change the scaling of the rendering using the .scale() function of the projection. The default value for scale is 150, and the corresponding values will make the rendering larger or smaller.

The following example makes the globe twice as large along with setting the center of the globe to not be clipped by the SVG container:

bl.ock (12.10): http://goo.gl/EVsHgU

```
var projection = d3.geo.orthographic()
    .scale(300)
    .clipAngle(90)
    .translate([width / 2, height / 2]);
```

This orthographic projection, by default, centers the view on the globe at latitude and longitude (**0,0**). If we want to center on another location, we need to .rotate() the projection by a number of degrees of latitude and longitude.

The following example rotates the globe to show the United States prominently:

bl.ock (12.11): http://goo.gl/1acSjF

The one change to the projection is the following:

```
var projection = d3.geo.orthographic()
    .scale(300)
    .clipAngle(90)
    .translate([width / 2, height / 2])
    .rotate([90, -40]);
```

This change in the projection gives us the following result:

Spicing up a globe

Although this globe is quite impressive for the amount of code used to create it, it feels a little dull. Let's differentiate the countries a little more, and also add the lines of latitude and longitude.

Coloring the countries on a globe

We can color the countries on the globe using a `d3.scale.category20()` color scale. But we can't simply rotate through the colors, as there will be cases where adjacent countries will be filled with the same color.

To avoid this, we will take advantage of another function of TopoJSON, `topojson.` `neighbors()`. This function will return, given a set of geometries (like the countries), a data structure that identifies which geometries are adjacent to each other. We can then utilize this data to prevent the potential problem with colors.

The process is demonstrated in the following example:

bl.ock (12.12): `http://goo.gl/9UimER`

The projection in this example remains the same. The remainder of the code is changed.

We start by using the same projection as the last example so that code is not repeated here. The following creates the data structure of the colors, the countries, and the neighbors:

```
var color = d3.scale.category20();
var countries = topojson.feature(world,
                        world.objects.countries).features;
var neighbors = topojson.neighbors(
                        world.objects.countries.geometries);
```

The creation of the globe then uses the following statement:

```
var color = d3.scale.category20();
svg.selectAll('.country')
    .data(countries)
    .enter()
    .append('path')
    .attr('d', path)
    .style('fill', function (d, i) {
        return color(d.color = d3.max(neighbors[i],
            function (n) {
                return countries[n].color;
            })
            + 1 | 0);
    });
```

Our resulting globe is the following:

Pretty nice! But it's still lacking in the lines of longitude or latitude, and you can't really tell what the extents of the globe are. Let's fix that now by adding the lines of latitude and longitude.

You'll be really surprised at how easy it is to add the latitudes and longitudes. In D3.js, these are referred to as **graticules**. We create them by instantiating a `d3.geo.graticules()` object, and then by appending a separate path prior to the path for the countries.

This is demonstrated in the following example:

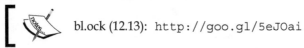

bl.ock (12.13): `http://goo.gl/5eJOai`

The only code added to the previous example is the following:

```
var graticule = d3.geo.graticule();
svg.append('path')
    .datum(graticule)
    .attr('d', path)
    .style({
        fill: 'none',
        stroke: '#777',
        'stroke-width': '.5px',
        'stroke-opacity': 0.5
    });
```

The change in code results in the following:

Voila! And as they say, easy-peasy!

Adding interactivity to maps

What good is a map if the user is not able to pan and zoom around the map to change the focus, and take a closer look at things? Fortunately, because of D3.js, this becomes very simple to implement. We will look at three different examples of interactivity and maps:

- Panning and zooming a world map
- Highlighting country borders on `mouseover`
- Rotating a globe with the mouse

Panning and zooming a world map

To demonstrate panning and zooming of a world map, we will make a few modifications to our world Mercator projection example. These modifications will be for using the mouse wheel to zoom in and out, and to be able to drag the map to move it to another center.

A possible image with this version of the map code could look like the following, which is centered just east of Brazil, and brought up several factors of zoom:

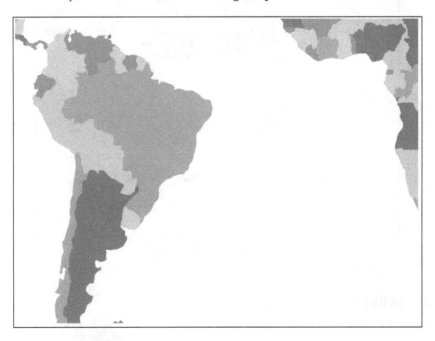

There are a couple of considerations that we should take into account when panning and zooming a map:

- We can only zoom in and out between two extents so that we do not zoom out too far as to lose sight of the map, or too close as to get lost in a single country

- We can only drag the map to a certain extent to ensure that it is constrained and not dragged off some edge

The example is available at the following location:

bl.ock (12.14): `http://goo.gl/jjouGK`

Much of the code is reused from the Mercator projection example, and also adds the code to uniquely color the countries.

The creation of the main SVG element differs to allow for drag and zoom. This starts with creating a zoom behavior, and assigning it to the main SVG element. Additionally, since we need to zoom the client elements, we add a group to facilitate this action:

```
var zoom = d3.behavior.zoom()
    .scaleExtent([1, 5])
    .on('zoom', moveAndZoom);

var svg = d3.select('body')
    .append('svg')
    .attr({
        width: width,
        height: height
    })
    .call(zoom);
var mainGroup = svg.append('g');
```

The rest of the main part of the code loads the data and renders the map, and is identical to the previous examples.

The `moveAndZoom` function, which will be called on any drag and zoom events, is given as follows:

```
function moveAndZoom() {
    var t = d3.event.translate;
    var s = d3.event.scale;

    var x = Math.min(
        (width / height) * (s - 1),
        Math.max(width * (1 - s), t[0]));

    var h = height / 4;
    var y = Math.min(
        h * (s - 1) + h * s,
        Math.max(height * (1 - s) - h * s, t[1]));

    mainGroup.attr('transform', 'translate(' + x + ',' + y +
                                    ')scale(' + s + ')');
}
```

From these values, we need to adjust the SVG translate on the map based upon the current mouse position, while taking into account the scale level. We also do not want this to translate the map in any direction such that there is padding between the map and the boundaries; this is handled by combined calls to `Math.min` and `Math.max`.

Congratulations, you now have a fully pan and scan map!

> Note that as you zoom in, the boundaries on the countries are fairly ragged. This is due to the 110-meter resolution of the data. To have more accurate graphics, use the files with the finer details. Even better, dynamically change to higher resolution data depending upon the zoom level.

Highlighting country borders on mouse hover

Now let's add another interactivity effect to our map: highlighting the border of a country which has the mouse currently over its geometry. This will help us accentuate the country the user is currently examining. A quick demonstration of this is the following, where Peru has a thin white border:

The example is available at the following location:

bl.ock (12.15): `http://goo.gl/DTtJ2A`

This is implemented with a few modifications to the previous example. The modifications start with the creation of the top-level group element:

```
mainGroup.style({
    stroke: 'white',
    'stroke-width': 2,
    'stroke-opacity': 0.0
});
```

This code informs D3.js that all SVG elements contained within the group will have a 2-pixel white border, which is initially transparent. When we hover the mouse, we will make this visible on the appropriate geometry.

Now we need to hook up mouse event handlers on each of the path elements that represent countries. On the `mouseover` event, we make the `stroke-opacity` opaque, and set it back to transparent when the mouse exits:

```
mainGroup.selectAll('path')
    .on('mouseover', function () {
        d3.select(this).style('stroke-opacity', 1.0);
    });
mainGroup.selectAll('path')
    .on('mouseout', function () {
        d3.select(this).style('stroke-opacity', 0.0);
    });
```

There is one more small change that we will want to make whenever the zoom level changes. As the zoom level goes up, the country borders get disproportionately thick. To prevent this, we can add the following statement to the end of the moveAndZoom function:

```
g.style("stroke-width", ((1 / s) * 2) + "px");
```

This is stating that the border of a country should always stay at what is visually 2px thick, no matter what the zoom level.

Rotating a globe using the mouse

Interactivity can also be applied to other projections. We will examine rotating an orthographic globe using the mouse. The example is available at the following location:

[bl.ock (12.16): `http://goo.gl/cpH0LN`]

To save a little space, we won't show an image here, as it looks the same as the earlier example in the chapter, except that it rotates following the mouse. That, and the rotation effect is lost in a print medium.

But the way this works is very simple. The technique involves creating two scales, one for longitude and the other for latitude. Longitude is calculated as mapping the mouse position from 0 to the width of the graphic to -180 and 180 degrees of longitude. The latitude is a mapping of the vertical mouse position to 90 and -90 degrees:

```
var scaleLongitude = d3.scale.linear()
    .domain([0, width])
    .range([-180, 180]);

var scaleLatitude = d3.scale.linear()
    .domain([0, height])
    .range([90, -90]);
```

When the mouse is moved over the SVG element, we capture it and scale the mouse position into a corresponding latitude and longitude; we then set the rotation of the projection:

```
svg.on('mousemove', function() {
    var p = d3.mouse(this);
    projection.rotate([scaleLongitude(p[0]),
                        scaleLatitude(p[1])]);
    svg.selectAll('path').attr('d', path);
});
```

It's a pretty cool little trick of mathematics and scales that allows us to be able to see every position on the entire globe.

Annotating a map

Our final examples of working with maps will demonstrate making annotations to a map. The first two will demonstrate placing labels and markers on a map, and the third will demonstrate the use of gradient colors to color regions all the way down to a state level.

All of these techniques would normally involve some fairly complex math if we had to do it on our own, but thankfully, D3.js again comes to help us solve this with just a few statements.

Labelling states using centroids

The maps of the United States we've created up to this point feel a little lacking in content, as they have not had the names of the states placed over their geometries. It would be very helpful to many reading a map to have the names visible. The example is available at the following location:

bl.ock (12.17): `http://goo.gl/3vChcR`

The result of the example is the following:

This is actually fairly easy to implement, with only the addition of one statement to our United States Mercator projection example. The following code is placed immediately after the `.selectAll()` statement that creates the boundaries for all the states:

```
svg.selectAll('text')
    .data(data.features)
    .enter()
    .append('text')
    .text(function(d) { return d.properties.name; })
    .attr({
        x: function(d) { return path.centroid(d)[0]; },
        y: function(d) { return path.centroid(d)[1]; },
        'text-anchor': 'middle',
        'font-size': '6pt'
    });
```

This statement creates a text element for each geometric feature in the data file, and sets the text to be the value of the name property of the geometry object.

The position of the text uses a function of the path that calculates the **centroid** of the geometry. The centroid is the mathematical center of the geometry, and can be calculated using the .centroid() function of a path.

For most states, especially rectangular ones, this works well. For others with irregular shapes, take Michigan for example, the placement is perhaps not optimal for aesthetics. There are various ways to fix this, but those are beyond the scope of this book (a hint: it involves adding additional data to represent location offsets for each geometry).

Placing symbols at specific geographic locations

The last example with maps that we will look at will be to place SVG elements on the map at specific coordinates. Specifically, we will place circles at the position of the 50 most populous cities, and size the circle relative to the population.

The data we will use is in us-cities.csv, which is available at https://gist.githubusercontent.com/d3byex/65a128a9a499f7f0b37d/raw/176771c2f08db d3431009ae27bef9b2f2fb56e36/us-cities.csv. The data is straightforward; the following are the first few lines:

```
name,population,latitude,longitude
New York,8491079,40.6643,-73.9385
Los Angeles,3792621,34.0194,-118.4108
Chicago,2695598,41.8376,-87.6818
```

The example is available at the following location:

bl.ock (12.18): http://goo.gl/Y9MN5q

The resulting visualization is the following:

The preceding example leverages the United States Mercator examples code. This example does, however, need to load two data files. To facilitate this, we will use a library called **queue** created by Mike Bostock to load these files asyncronously, and when both are complete, execute the `ready()` function. You can get this library and documentation at `https://github.com/mbostock/queue`:

```
queue()
    .defer(d3.json, usDataUrl)
    .defer(d3.csv, citiesDataUrl)
    .await(function (error, states, cities) {
```

The map is then rendered as in the earlier examples. Then we need to place the circles. To do this, we will need to convert the latitude and longitude values to X and Y pixel locations. We can do this in D3.js using the projection object:

```
svg.selectAll('circle')
    .data(cities)
    .enter()
    .append('circle')
    .each(function(d) {
        var location = projection([d.longitude, d.latitude]);
        d3.select(this).attr({
            cx: location[0],
            cy: location[1],
            r: Math.sqrt(+d.population * 0.00004)
        });
    })
    .style({
        fill: 'blue',
        opacity: 0.75
    });
```

For each circle that is created, this code calls the projection function passing it the latitude and longitude for each city. The return value is the x and y location of the pixel representing that location. So we just set the center of the circle to this result, and assign the circle a radius that is a scale value of the population.

Creating a choropleth

Our last map example is for creating a **choropleth**. A choropleth is a map with areas filled in with different colors to reflect the underlying data values — not just differing colors to represent different geographic boundaries. These are quite common types of visuals, and they commonly show a difference in opinion amongst the populations in adjacent regions, or how economic factors differ along neighbors.

The example is available at the following location:

bl.ock (12.19): `http://goo.gl/ZeTh4o`

The resulting visualization is the following:

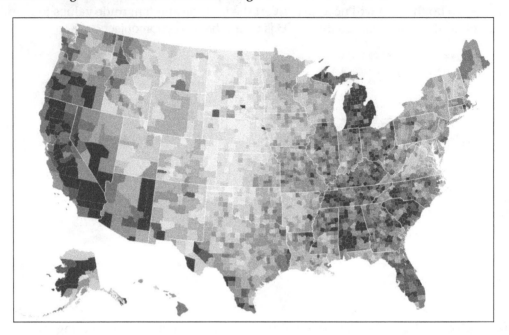

This choropleth represents the unemployment rate in the US counties for the year 2008. The shade of blue varies from darker, representing lower unemployment, to lighter and higher unemployment.

The data for unemployment is available at `https://gist.githubusercontent.com/d3byex/65a128a9a499f7f0b37d/raw/176771c2f08dbd3431009ae27bef9b2f2fb56e36/unemployment.tsv`. The first few lines are the following:

```
id     rate
1001   .097
1003   .091
1005   .134
1007   .121
1009   .099
1011   .164
```

The data consists of a pair of a county identifier and the respective unemployment rate. The county ID will be matched to county IDs in the `us.json` file available at `https://gist.githubusercontent.com/d3byex/65a128a9a499f7f0b37d/raw/176771c2f08dbd3431009ae27bef9b2f2fb56e36/us.json`.

This file consists of TopoJSON describing the shape of all of the counties in the US, each with the same county ID in the unemployment file. A snippet of this file is the following, which shows for country `1001` the arcs that should be used to render it:

```
{
  "type": "Polygon",
  "id": 1001,
  "arcs": [ [ -8063, 8094, 8095, -8084, -7911 ] ]
},
```

Our goal is to quantize the unemployment rates, and then fill each geometry with a color mapped to that quantile. It's actually easier to do than it may seem.

In this example, we will map our unemployment rates into ten quantiles. The color used for each will be specified using a style with a specific name. These are declared as follows:

```
<style>
    .q0-9 { fill:rgb(247,251,255); }
    .q1-9 { fill:rgb(222,235,247); }
    .q2-9 { fill:rgb(198,219,239); }
    .q3-9 { fill:rgb(158,202,225); }
    .q4-9 { fill:rgb(107,174,214); }
    .q5-9 { fill:rgb(66,146,198); }
    .q6-9 { fill:rgb(33,113,181); }
    .q7-9 { fill:rgb(8,81,156); }
    .q8-9 { fill:rgb(8,48,107); }
</style>
```

The data is loaded using the `queue()` function:

```
queue()
    .defer(d3.json, usDataUrl)
    .defer(d3.tsv, unempDataUrl, function(d) {
                        rateById.set(d.id, +d.rate);
    })
    .await(function(error, us) {
```

This code uses an alternate form of `.defer()` for the unemployment data, which calls a function for each data item that is loaded (another cool thing about queue). This builds a `d3.map()` object (like a dictionary object) that maps the county ID to its unemployment rate, and we use this map later during rendering.

The county data is rendered first. To do this, we need to create a quantile scale which maps the domain from 0 to 0.15. This will be used to map the unemployment levels to one of the styles. The range is then configured to generate the names of the nine styles:

```
var quantize = d3.scale.quantize()
    .domain([0, .15])
    .range(d3.range(9).map(function(i) {
        return 'q' + i + '-9';
    }));
```

Next, the code creates the albersUsa projection and an associated path:

```
var projection = d3.geo.albersUsa()
    .scale(1280)
    .translate([width / 2, height / 2]);

var path = d3.geo.path()
    .projection(projection);
```

The next step is to create a group to hold the shaded counties. Then, to this group, we will add a path for each county by binding it to the counties features:

```
svg.append('g')
    .attr('class', "counties")
    .selectAll("path")
    .data(topojson.feature(us, us.objects.counties).features)
    .enter()
    .append("path")
    .attr("class", function(d) {
        return quantize(rateById.get(d.id));
    })
    .attr("d", path);
```

Finally, we overlay the outlines of the states using a white stroke for the borders to help us differentiate the state borders:

```
svg.append('path')
    .datum(topojson.mesh(us, us.objects.states)
    .attr({
        'class': 'states',
        fill: 'none',
        stroke: '#fff',
        'stroke-linejoin': 'round',
        'd': path
    });
```

This particular piece of code also uses the topojson.mesh function to extract the **MultiPolygon** (GeoJSON) data for all of the states from the TopoJSON object.

And that's all! We've created a choropleth, and used a coding pattern that can be reused easily with other types of data.

Summary

We started this chapter by looking briefly at GeoJSON and TopoJSON. If you do anything with maps in D3.js, you will be using one or both of these. We covered it just enough to give an understanding of its structure, and how it is used to define data that can be rendered as a map.

From there, we dove into creating several maps and covered many of the concepts that you will use in their creation. These included loading the data, creating projections, and rendering the geometries within the data.

We examined two projections, Mercator and orthographic, to give an idea of how these present data. Along the way, we also looked at how to style elements on the map, filling geometries with color, and highlighting geometries on mouseover.

Then we examined how to annotate our maps with labels as well as color elements based upon data (choropleths), and to place symbols on the map at specific geographic positions, with a size that is based upon the data.

At this point in the book, we have been pretty thorough in covering much of the core of D3.js, at least enough to make you very dangerous with it. But we have also only ever created stand-alone visualizations, ones that do not interact with other visualizations.

In the next chapter, the final one of this book, we will look at combining multiple D3.js visualizations using AngularJS, and where those visuals also react to the user manipulating other content on their page.

13
Combining D3.js and AngularJS

The final topic in this book will demonstrate using multiple D3.js visuals on a single web page. These examples will also demonstrate constructing D3.js visuals in a modular manner, which allows their reuse through simple HTML tags, and at the same time abstracting the data from the code that renders the visual. This will enable the creation of more generic D3.js visuals, which can be placed on a page using a single HTML tag and are also loosely coupled with the source of the data.

To implement these features, we will utilize **AngularJS**, a JavaScript framework used to create dynamic and modular web applications. The examples will demonstrate how to integrate both AngularJS (v1.4) and D3.js to make reusable and interoperable visualizations. An introductory knowledge of AngularJS is expected for this chapter, but the focus will be on how to use the features of AngularJS to create reusable and extensible D3.js controls; therefore, even someone new to AngularJS will be able to follow along.

In this chapter, we will accomplish this by going through the following topics:

- An overview of composite visualization
- Creating a bar chart using an AngularJS application, controller, and directive
- Adding a second directive to add a donut graph to the page
- Adding a detail view and interactivity between the visuals
- Updating the graphs upon modification of details in the data

An overview of composite visualization

Before jumping into the examples, let's start by examining the end result to help conceptualize several of the goals that we will attempt to accomplish using AngularJS combined with D3.js. The following figure represents a static image of the resulting interactive and composite graphs:

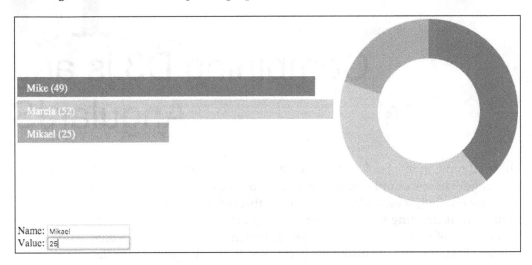

Each component of the page—the bar graph, the donut graph, and the input form—will initially be built independently and will be able to function on its own. To do this, the examples will use features from AngularJS to facilitate the following features:

- Each visual should be expressed in HTML as a simple HTML tag instead of copying the code for each onto the page. This is performed using AngularJS directives.

- Instead of loading the data once within the code for each visual, we will leverage a common application-level data model shared across each element. In AngularJS, this is done by creating a JavaScript data model and injecting it into the controllers for each directive.

- The bar graph will provide a means of exposing notifications of updates to a currently selected item, upon which the detail model can update its data. This will be implemented through a selectedItem property in the model that the details directive can monitor for updates using AngularJS template bindings.

- Also, when the application model is updated in the details directive, the bar and donut graphs will be notified by AngularJS to be updated to represent the modifications.

A note of difference in this chapter from the previous is that the code is not available online on bl.ock.org or JSBIN.COM and must be retrieved from the Packt website. This is because the examples utilize AngularJS, which doesn't play as well with bl.ock.org and JSBIN.COM. The code must therefore be run locally from a web server. You can simply unzip the code and place it in the root of a web server or start a web server of your choice in the root folder of the content. Each example is implemented as a different HTML file in the root of the folder, and each of these refers to multiple other files in various subdirectories.

Creating a bar graph using AngularJS

The first example will create a reusable bar chart component to demonstrate creating an AngularJS directive with an underlying controller. This is implemented within an HTML file, `01_just_bars.html`, which consists of the following components:

- **The AngularJS application object:** This functions as an entry point for AngularJS code in the page (that is, in `app.js`)

- An AngularJS controller (in `controllers/basic_dashboard.js`): This creates the data and sends it to the directive that renders the HTML code for the graph

- The directive: This renders the D3.js bar chart in `directives/bars.js`.

The web page and application

The AngularJS application is presented to the user via a web page, which begins by loading the AngularJS and D3.js libraries (this is common in all the examples in this chapter). Take a look at the following code:

```
<script src="https://ajax.googleapis.com/ajax/libs/angularjs/1.2.10/
angular.min.js"></script>
<script src="http://d3js.org/d3.v3.min.js" charset="utf-8"></script>
```

The page then loads the implementations of the AngularJS application object, directive, and controller. Now, execute the following code:

```
<script src="app.js"></script>
<script src="directives/bars.js"></script>
<script src="controllers/basic_dashboard.js"></script>
```

The details of these will be examined in a moment. Before we look at these, the remainder of the HTML code in this file creates the AngularJS application and the controller for our directive using a `<div>` tag with the `ng-app` and `ng-controller` properties. Add the following code:

```
<div ng-app="dashboardApp" ng-controller="dashboardController">
    <bars-view width="500" height="105"></bars-view>
</div>
```

The use of the `ng-app` attribute tells AngularJS where to find the implementation, which is a module (that is, a piece of AngularJS JavaScript referable) named `dashboardApp`.

In this example, this module is declared in `app.js` (this is the same for each example):

```
angular.module('dashboardApp', []);
```

This example does not actually declare any code for the application module and is simply a place for the HTML markup to reach into AngularJS and start locating various objects. In a more elaborate application, this would be a good place to inject other dependent modules and do some application-level initialization.

The tag within this `<div>` tag defines a construct known as an AngularJS directive. This renders the data represented in the controller. Before we get to the implementation of the directive, let's take a look at the controller that provides the data to the directive.

The controller

The `ng-controller` attribute on the `<div>` tag specifies a name of a controller that is used to provide data to the AngularJS directives that are specified as the child elements of this `<div>` tag. AngularJS searches for a controller with the specified name within one of the modules specified by `ng-app`. In this example, this controller is declared in `controllers/basic_dashboard.js`, as follows:

```
angular.module('dashboardApp')
    .controller('dashboardController',
        ['$scope', function ($scope) {
            $scope.items = [
                { Name: 'Mike', Value: 49 },
                { Name: 'Marcia', Value: 52 },
                { Name: 'Mikael', Value: 18 }
            ];
        }]);
```

This creates an AngularJS controller using `.controller()` with the name `dashboardController`, which is a part of the application's `dashboardApp` module. Take a look at the following script:

```
angular.module('dashboardApp')
        .controller('dashboardController',
                    ['$scope', function ($scope) {
```

The second parameter of `.controller()` is an array that specifies the variables to be injected into the method implementing the controller and then the function that implements the controller.

Now, this informs AngularJS that we would like the AngularJS variable `$scope`, which represents the data of the controller and will be injected into the directives of the control to be passed into this function that is to be initialized.

The last statement in the following command declares the data that is to be provided to the view by adding an item's property to the scope:

```
$scope.items = [
    { Name: 'Mike', Value: 49 },
    { Name: 'Marcia', Value: 52 },
    { Name: 'Mikael', Value: 18 }
];
```

The directive for a bar graph

An angular directive is a custom HTML tag that instructs AngularJS on how to create HTML based on the data provided by the controller. In the HTML code of the example is a tag declared that is named `<bars-view>`. When loading the page, AngularJS examines all the tags in HTML, and if a tag is not recognized as a standard HTML tag, AngularJS searches for a directive that you declared as part of the application to provide an implementation for this tag.

In this case, it converts the hyphenated name of the tag, `<bars-view>`, to a camel case version, `barsView`, and looks for a directive within a module that was declared with this name. If found, AngularJS executes the code that is provided for the directive to generate the HTML code.

In this example, AngularJS finds the `<bars-view>` tag implemented in the `directives/bars.js` file. This file starts by informing AngularJS that we want to declare a directive named `barsView` in the `dashboardApp` module:

```
angular.module('dashboardApp')
    .directive('barsView', function () {
        return {
            restrict: 'E',
            scope: { data: '=' },
            link: renderView
        };
```

The second parameter to `.directive()` is a function that informs AngularJS how to apply and construct the view. In this example, there are three instructions specified:

- `restrict: 'E'`: This informs AngularJS that this directive applies to HTML elements only and not to their attributes or CSS class names.
- `scope: { data: "="}`: This tells AngularJS that we want to have **two-way binding** between the data in the scope and the elements in the view. If data changes in the controller, AngularJS will update the view and vice versa.
- `link: renderView`: This property informs AngularJS which function will be called when the view is created. This function will then generate DOM constructs to represent the view. This is where we will put our D3.js code.

The `renderView` function is declared as follows:

```
function renderView($scope, $elements, $attrs) {
```

When AngularJS calls this function to render a tag for a directive, it passes the scope object represented by the related controller as the `$scope` parameter. The second parameter, `$elements`, is passed an AngularJS object that can be used to identify the top-level DOM element where the directive should append new elements. The last parameter, `$attrs`, is passed any custom attribute defined in the root DOM element in the prior parameter.

The code to implement the bar graph is not significantly different from our earlier bar graph examples. The first thing it does that is different because of AngularJS gets the data from the scope that was passed into the function, as follows:

```
var data = $scope.$parent.items;
```

The `<bars-view>` directive is assigned a scope object by AngularJS. The data from the controller is actually a property of the `parent` scope property of this object. This object has the `items` property that we defined in the controller and its associated data as the `items` property.

The width and height of the element, as specified in the HTML code, can be retrieved using the `width` and `height` attributes of the `$attrs` parameter. Take a look at the following command:

```
var width = $attrs.width, height = $attrs.height;
```

After obtaining the width and height, we can create the main SVG element of the graph. This will be appended to `$element[0]`, which represents the root DOM element for this directive (The `$element` object is actually an AngularJS one wrapping the root element, which is access using the `[0]` indexer), as follows:

```
var svg = d3.select($element[0])
    .append("svg");
```

The remainder of the code is similar to the examples covered in previous chapters to create a bar graph with overlaid text. It begins by setting the size of the SVG element and setting up various variables required to calculate the size and positions of the bars, as shown in the following code:

```
svg.attr({
    width: width,
    height: height
});

var max = d3.max(data, function(d) {
    return d.Value;
});

var colors = d3.scale.category20();

var barHeight = 30;
var leftMargin = 15;
var barTextOffsetY = 22;
```

The bars are then created and set to animate to their maximum respective sizes. Take a look at the following:

```
svg.selectAll('rect')
    .data(data)
    .enter()
    .append('rect')
    .attr({
        height: barHeight,
        width: 0,
        x: 0,
        y: function(d, i) {
```

```
                return i * barHeight;
            },
            stroke: 'white'
        })
        .style('fill', function(d, i) {
            return colors(i);
        })
        .transition()
        .duration(1000)
        .attr('width', function(d) {
            return d.Value / (max / width);
        });
```

Now, all the existing D3.js elements are selected in an update scenario, which transitions the size of any existing bar to the new size. Take a look at this code:

```
svg.selectAll("rect")
    .data(data)
    .transition()
    .duration(1000)
    .attr("width", function(d, i) {
        return d.Value / (max / width);
    });
```

Then, the cases to create both the entering labels on the bars and change the text on the bars if the data values change are implemented, as follows:

```
svg.selectAll('text')
    .data(data)
    .enter()
    .append('text')
    .attr({
        fill: '#fff',
        x: leftMargin,
        y: function(d, i) {
            return i * barHeight + barTextOffsetY;
        }
    })
    .text(function(d) {
        return d.Name + ' (' + d.Value + ')';
    });

svg.selectAll('text')
    .data(data)
    .attr({
```

```
        fill: '#fff',
        x: leftMargin,
        y: function(d, i) {
            return i * barHeight + barTextOffsetY;
        }
    })
    .text(function(d) {
        return d.Name + ' (' + d.Value + ')';
    });
}
```

When opening this page in the browser, the following graph is presented:

Adding a second directive for a donut

The next example adds a second D3.js visualization to represent a donut graph of the values in the data. This implementation requires creating a new directive and adding this directive to the web page. It reuses the implementation of the controller and also the data that it creates.

The web page

The web page for this example is available in 02_bars_and_donut.html. The web page is slightly different from the previous one in that it includes one additional view for the donut. Take a look at the following:

```
<script src="app.js"></script>
<script src="views/bars.js"></script>
<script src="views/donut.js"></script>
<script src="controllers/basic_dashboard.js"></script>
```

The declaration of the content for the page now becomes the following:

```
<div ng-app="dashboardApp" ng-controller="BasicBarsController">
    <bars-view width="500" height="105"
               style="display: table-cell; vertical-align: middle">
    </bars-view>
    <donut-view width="300" height="300"
                style="display: table-cell">
    </donut-view>
</div>
```

This adds an additional directive for donut-view. There is also a style added to the directives to make them float next to each other.

The directive for the donut graph

The implementation of the donut directive begins by declaring that that this directive will be added to the dashboardApp module and that its name will be donutView (hence we use <donut-view> in the HTML code). As with the bar graph directive, it also instructs AngularJS that this code should be applied only to DOM elements, have two-way data binding, and be implemented by a function named renderView; take a look at the following code:

```
angular.module('dashboardApp')
    .directive('donutView', function () {
        return {
            restrict: 'E',
            scope: { data: '=' },
            link: renderView
        };
```

This version of renderView follows a similar pattern to the implementation for bars-view. It begins by getting the data from the scope, including the width and height of the visual, and also calculates the radius for the donut. The following code is executed:

```
function renderView($scope, $elements, $attrs) {
    var data = $scope.$parent.items;

    var width = $attrs.width,
        height = $attrs.height,
        radius = Math.min(width, height) / 2;
```

The rendering of the donut is then started using a pie layout, as follows:

```
var pie = d3.layout.pie()
    .value(function (d) { return d.Value; })
    .sort(null);
```

The arcs fill between 10 and 70 pixels from the outside of the boundary of the SVG element, which is based on the calculated radius. Take a look at the following code:

```
var arc = d3.svg.arc()
    .innerRadius(radius - 70)
    .outerRadius(radius - 10);
```

Then, the visual is started to be constructed by appending the main SVG element to $elements[0], as follows:

```
var svg = d3.select($elements[0])
    .append('svg')
    .attr({
        width: width,
        height: height
});
```

Finally, the visual elements for the donut graph are constructed using a color scale and path generator for each entering datum, as follows:

```
var colors = d3.scale.category20();
graphGroup
    .datum(data)
    .selectAll('path')
    .data(pie)
    .enter()
    .append('path')
    .attr('fill', function(d, i) {
        return colors(i);
    })
    .attr('d', arc)
    .each(function(d) {
        this._current = d;
    });
```

Upon loading this page in the browser, it presents the following visual, which now has two D3.js visuals on a single web page:

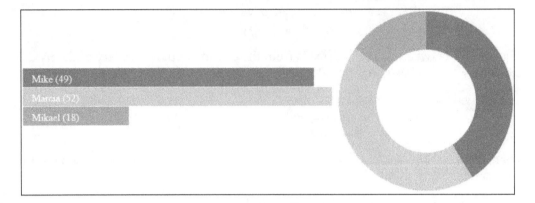

Adding a detail view and interactivity

The next example adds a details directive to the page and also interactivity such that when a bar is clicked, the details directive will display the appropriate data for the selected bar.

To achieve this interactivity, the bar graph directive is modified so that it produces an action that can be monitored by other parts of the AngularJS application. This action will be to set a `selectedItem` property on the model, which other controllers or directives can watch for changes and then take action.

The web page

The web page for this example is contained in `03_with_detail.html`. The content included differs slightly, in that we will include a new implementation of our `<bars-view>` directive in `directives/bars_with_click.js` and the controller in `controllers/enhanced_controller.js` and a reference to a new directive representing the detail view in `directives/detail.js`. Take a look at the following:

```
<script src="app.js"></script>
<script src="directives/bars_with_click.js"></script>
<script src="directives/donut.js"></script>
<script src="directives/detail.js"></script>
<script src="controllers/enhanced_controller.js">
</script>
```

The declaration of the main <div> tag changes slightly to the following by adding a directive for details-view:

```
<div ng-app="dashboardApp" ng-controller="dashboardController">
    <bars-view width="500" height="105"
        style="display: table-cell; vertical-align: middle">
    </bars-view>
    <donut-view width="300" height="300"
        style="display: table-cell"></donut-view>
    <details-view data="selectedItem" width="300">
    </details-view>
</div>
```

Note that this new directive uses an attribute named data and sets its value to selectedItem. This is a special AngularJS attribute/binding that specifies that the model data for this directive will be located in the selectedItem property of the nearest scope object upward in the DOM hierarchy. In this case, it is the scope defined on the div tag, and whenever this property on the scope is changed, this directive will update its data and visualization automatically.

Specifying an initial selectedItem in the controller

The details view controller expects to have access to a selectedItem property of the model to use as its data, and it will, therefore, need to set an initial value to this property. The following adds a single line to accomplish this task:

```
angular.module('dashboardApp')
    .controller('dashboardController',
                ['$scope', function ($scope) {
        $scope.items = [
            { Name: 'Mike', Value: 49 },
            { Name: 'Marcia', Value: 52 },
            { Name: 'Mikael', Value: 18 }
        ];
        $scope.selectedItem = $scope.items[0];
    }]);
```

The modified bars view directive

The `<bars-view>` directive then adds a click handler to set the value of the selected item whenever a bar is clicked, as follows:

```
.on('click', function (d, i) {
    $timeout(function () {
        parent.selectedItem = d;
    };
})
```

This click handler performs one action: it updates the value of the selected item in the parent scope to the value of the data item underlying the clicked visual. It does not send messages to other components, nor should it. Other directives, if interested in this update, will be able to take this action by looking for changes in the model.

 This is wrapped in a call to the AngularJS $timeout function, which will have the browser update the UI, based on the change of this property. If this is not performed, any interested element will not by notified by AngularJS.

Implementing the details view directive

The details view is a fairly simple piece of code that starts with a directive declaration. Take a look at the following:

```
angular.module('dashboardApp')
    .directive('detailsView', function () {
        return {
            restrict: 'E',
            scope: { data: "=" },
            templateUrl: 'templates/static_item.html'
        };
    });
```

A difference in this declaration from our other directives is that the code does not specify a `link` property but a `templateUrl` property and an associated value. This tells AngularJS that this directive will not be implemented by a call to a JavaScript function but should use content from the `templates/static_item.html` file. The contents of this file are the following:

```
Name: {{data.Name}}
<br/>
Value: {{data.Value}}
```

This HTML code will be injected into DOM by AngularJS. The HTML contains embedded **handlebars** syntax that AngularJS will notice and substitute the content of. In this case, the values of the Name and Value properties of the object specified by the data attribute of the directive will be used, where data is the bound value of selectedItem from the model, which is the currently selected bar. Whenever this property is updated, AngularJS will automatically update DOM correctly on our behalf without any additional coding.

The resulting interactive page

The following image is an example of a possible display rendered by this page:

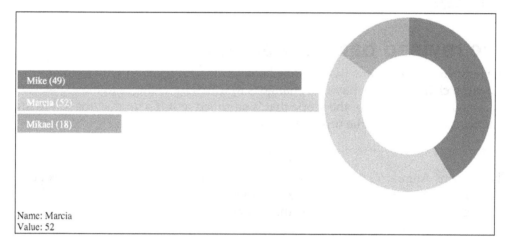

In this image, the second bar was clicked on, and so the details view displays the data for this bar. As you click on the different bars, the values in the details change to match.

Updating graphs upon the modification of details data

The final example will make the update of the data bidirectional between the details view and bar and donut graphs. The previous example only updates the detail view upon clicking on a bar. The content of the details view is static text, and hence, the user cannot modify the data. This is changed by modifying the template to utilize text input fields. There is no change to the controller, so it will not be discussed.

The web page

The web page for this example, 04_dynamic.html, contains several small changes from the previous example to reference new implementations for the bars, donut, and details directives. The <div> tag remains the same. Take a look at the following code:

```
<script src="app.js"></script>
<script src="directives/bars_with_click_and_updates.js"></script>
<script src="directives/donut_with_updates.js"></script>
<script src="directives/dynamic_detail.js"></script>
<script src="controllers/enhanced_controller.js">
</script>
```

The revised bar-view directive

The new <bar-view> directive has one behavioral change along with a small structural change. This behavioral change is to watch for changes to the selectedItem property of the scope that is supplied to it. To do this, the following statement is added near the top of the code for renderView():

```
parent.$watch("selectedItem", render, true);
```

This informs AngularJS that we want it to watch for changes in the bound scope object's selectedItem property. When this property or any property of this object changes (as specified by true as the third parameter), AngularJS will call the render() function.

 Note that this watch process does not have to be performed in the details view controller as the use of a template and handlebars sets this up automatically.

The structural change to the code is made after the call to select the svg element and the setting of its size. The code to create the visual is now wrapped in the new render() function, which is called the first time the directive is loaded and then each time the value of selectedItem is changed. When the latter happens, the bar graph is updated, it animates the bars to new sizes, and it also modifies the text labels.

The revised donut-view directive

Similarly to the updates to the `bar-view` directive, this directive is changed by adding a call to watch the `selectedItem` property of the scope as well as wrapping the rendering code in an `updatePath()` function, which can be called when the value of this property changes, as follows:

```
parent.$watch('selectedItem', updatePath, true);
```

The `updatePath()` function only needs to regenerate the path for each of the arc segments, as shown in the following code:

```
function updatePath() {
    path = path.data(pie);
    path.transition()
        .duration(750)
        .attrTween('d',
            function() {
                var i = d3.interpolate(this._current, a);
                this._current = i(0);
                return function(t) {
                    return arc(i(t));
                };
            });
}
```

The detail-view directive

The new `<detail-view>` directive has one modification, which is to use a different template. Take a look at the following code:

```
angular.module('dashboardApp')
    .directive('detailsView', function () {
        return {
            restrict: 'E',
            scope: { data: "=" },
            templateUrl: 'templates/dynamic_item.html'
        };
    });
```

The contents of this template specify input boxes instead of text fields, as follows:

```
Name: <input type="text" ng-model="data.Name"/>
<br/>
Value: <input type="text" ng-model="data.Value"/>
```

Note that for input fields to update handlebars, notations cannot be utilized. For this to work, you need to use the AngularJS `ng-model` attribute and point it to the bound data object and respective property.

The results

The following screenshot shows this example in action:

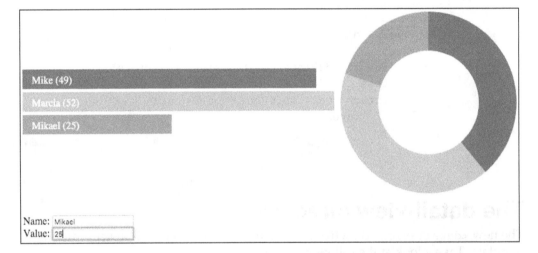

In this demonstration, the third bar was clicked on, and `details-view` now provides edit controls to allow us to change the values. The value for **Mikael** was then changed to **25**, and the bar and donut graphs were animated to represent the change in values.

One of the really nice things going on here is that literally, key stroke by key stroke on both of these input fields, AngularJS will update these properties and both the bar and donut charts will be updated on each key stroke!

Summary

The examples in this chapter demonstrated how to use AngularJS to make modular and composite D3.js visualizations. They started by showing how to place data within an AngularJS controller and share it with multiple D3.js visuals. Next, we demonstrated how to share data from a single controller to multiple directives. The final two examples demonstrated how to use a shared property for two-way communication and implement a details view to allow the editing of data.

This wraps up this book on using D3.js through examples. The book started with the basic concepts of D3.js and using its constructs to bind data and generate SVG from it. From this foundation, we progressed through adding features to the examples, each of which demonstrated progressive extensions of the previous examples within the same chapter as well as with incrementally complex constructs from chapter to chapter. In the end, the examples covered many of the concepts in D3.js that can take you from a novice to being able to construct rich, interactive, and composite visualizations, all through examples.

Index

Symbols

.enter() method
  entering elements, specifying with 29, 30
  used, for adding items 31, 32
.exit() method
  items, removing with 35, 36

A

albersUsa projection
  using 227, 228
AngularJS
  used, for creating bar graph 257
animated bubble plot
  URL 117
animated color
  URL 108
animation
  about 5, 108
  capabilities 108
  timers 116, 117
  transitions, using 108
arcs
  about 222
  generating 147-149
area path generator 146
axes
  about 66
  adding, to bar graph 75, 76
  creating 69-71
  labels, inverting 74
  orientation, modifying 72, 73

B

bar graph
  about 61
  axes, adding 75, 76
  creating 62, 63
  creating, AngularJS used 257
  enhancing, with interactivity 131-134
  labels, adding 64, 65
  margins, creating 66-68
  web page 257
basis interpolation
  used, for creating curved lines 158, 159
behaviors
  about 127
  drag 127
  zoom 127
behaviors module 6
binding 4
bl.ocks.org
  about 9
  URL 7, 9
  URL, for demonstration 9
bottom axis 69
bound 4
brushes
  online examples 135-137
  used, for highlighting selected items 135
  used, for implementing focus +
    context 138-142
bubble plot
  code, URL 104
  creating 103-105

E

ellipse **45**
entering elements
  specifying, with .enter() 29, 30
enter/update/exit pattern 23
Epicyclic Gearing bl.ock
  URL 11
exiting 38

F

feature collection 221
fields
  mapping 83, 84
fill color, rectangle
  animating 108, 109
flat map of world
  creating 230
fluent API 14
force-directed graphs
  about 197, 198
  example 200-203
  parameters 199
  parameters, URL 200
force-directed layouts 198

G

general update pattern 23, 37-39
GeoJSON
  about 217, 218
  US first map, creating 224-226
gist 9
GitHub
  about 7
  URL 7
globe
  countries, coloring 236-239
  rotating, with mouse 244, 245
  spicing up 236
Google Chrome 11, 12
gridlines
  adding, to scatter plots 100-102
  URL 100
groups, SVG elements 57

H

Hello World, D3.js style 12-14
hierarchal layouts
  about 172
  cluster dendrogram, creating 178-182
  hierarchy, representing with hierarchy
      diagram 183-185
  tree diagrams 172-178
hovering 125
HTML 1

I

information flow
  demonstrating 189
  representing, through multiple
      nodes 191-195
  streamgraphs, using 189-191
interaction 5
interpolators
  about 5, 114
  curved lines creating, basis interpolation
      used 158, 159
  curved lines creating, bundle interpolation
      used 160, 161
  curved lines creating, cardinal interpolation
      used 161
  linear-closed interpolators 156
  linear interpolators 156
  step before and step after
      interpolations 157
  used, for drawing line graphs 154-156
items
  adding, .enter() method used 31, 32
  removing, with .exit() method 35, 36

J

JavaScript Object Notation (JSON) 79
jQuery 3
Js Bin
  about 7, 8
  URL 7
JSON data
  loading 79, 80
  reference link 79

K

keyframes 108

L

layers, SVG elements 59
layouts module 6
linear-closed interpolators 157
linear interpolators 157
linear scales
  about 69, 85
  example 85
line graphs
  drawing, interpolators used 154-156
lines 46
link distance
  used, for spreading out nodes 204, 205
links
  directionality markers, adding 211-214
  styles, adding 211-214

M

map of world
  creating, Mercator projection used 231
maps
  annotating 245
  country borders, highlighting on mouse
    hover 242, 243
  interactivity, adding 240
  states labelling, centroids used 245-247
  symbols, placing at specific geographic
    locations 247, 248
  world map, panning 240-242
  world map, zooming 240-242
margin convention 67
margins
  about 66
  creating, in bar graph 66-68
mark 116
measurement 96
Mercator projection
  used, for creating map of world 231

modules
  about 6
  behaviors 6
  data-processing 6
  layouts 6
  scales 6
  shapes 6
mouse events
  handling 124
  mouse click, tracking 126
  mouse entering SVG element,
    capturing 125, 126
  mouse exiting SVG element,
    capturing 125, 126
  mouse position tracking, mousemove
    used 124, 125
mousemove
  used, for tracking mouse position 124, 125
multiple items
  style, changing of 19-22
multiple properties
  animating, simultaneously 110
  URL 110

N

nodes
  labelling, in layout 207, 208
  repulsion, adding for preventing crossed
    links 206, 207
  spreading out, link distance used 204, 205
  sticking 209, 210
numbers
  strings, converting 83, 84

O

ordinal scales
  about 86
  color strings, mapping to codes 86
  integers, mapping to colors scales 87, 88
  rangeBands, using 88, 89
  URL 88
orthographic projection
  spherical maps, creating with 233-236

P

pan 129-131
path data generators
  about 144
  arcs, creating 147
  area path generator 146
  curved lines creating, diagonals
       used 153, 154
  donuts, creating 147
  pie chart, creating 149, 150
  segments, creating 147
  sequence of lines, creating 144, 145
  symbols, creating 152, 153
  wedges, creating 147
paths
  about 46, 47
  commands 47
pie chart
  creating 149, 150
  pie, exploding 151
  ring graph, creating 152
points
  drawing, in scatter plots 96-98
polygon 219
Processing
  URL 3

R

rectangle 45
relationships
  representing, with chord diagrams 185-188
ring graph
  creating 152
rotate
  demonstrating 53, 54

S

Scalable Vector Graphics. *See* **SVG**
scale
  demonstrating 56
scale object 69
scales
  about 85
  linear scales 85

  ordinal scales 86
  viewership, visualizing 90-93
scales module 6
scatter plots
  creating 96
  example data, URL 96
  gridlines, adding 100-102
  points, plotting 96-98
  sprucing up 99
  with axes, URL 99
segments
  generating 147-149
selections 3, 4, 17, 18
shapes module 6
shapes, SVG
  about 45
  ellipse 45
  lines 46
  paths 46, 47
  rectangle 45
  text 47
spherical maps
  creating, with orthographic
      projection 233-236
stacked bar graph
  area graph, converting to expanded area
      graph 170, 171
  creating 164-168
  stacked bar, modifying 168, 170
stacked layouts
  using 163
step after interpolation 157, 158
step before interpolation 157, 158
streamgraphs
  using 189-191
strings
  converting, to numbers 83, 84
strokes 49-52
style
  changing, of DOM element 18, 19
  changing, of multiple items 19-22
SVG
  about 1, 41, 42
  attributes 42
  circles, drawing 43, 44
  coordinate system 42
  shapes 45

Thank you for buying
D3.js By Example

About Packt Publishing

Packt, pronounced 'packed', published its first book, *Mastering phpMyAdmin for Effective MySQL Management*, in April 2004, and subsequently continued to specialize in publishing highly focused books on specific technologies and solutions.

Our books and publications share the experiences of your fellow IT professionals in adapting and customizing today's systems, applications, and frameworks. Our solution-based books give you the knowledge and power to customize the software and technologies you're using to get the job done. Packt books are more specific and less general than the IT books you have seen in the past. Our unique business model allows us to bring you more focused information, giving you more of what you need to know, and less of what you don't.

Packt is a modern yet unique publishing company that focuses on producing quality, cutting-edge books for communities of developers, administrators, and newbies alike. For more information, please visit our website at www.packtpub.com.

About Packt Open Source

In 2010, Packt launched two new brands, Packt Open Source and Packt Enterprise, in order to continue its focus on specialization. This book is part of the Packt Open Source brand, home to books published on software built around open source licenses, and offering information to anybody from advanced developers to budding web designers. The Open Source brand also runs Packt's Open Source Royalty Scheme, by which Packt gives a royalty to each open source project about whose software a book is sold.

Writing for Packt

We welcome all inquiries from people who are interested in authoring. Book proposals should be sent to author@packtpub.com. If your book idea is still at an early stage and you would like to discuss it first before writing a formal book proposal, then please contact us; one of our commissioning editors will get in touch with you.

We're not just looking for published authors; if you have strong technical skills but no writing experience, our experienced editors can help you develop a writing career, or simply get some additional reward for your expertise.

open source*
community experience distilled

Mastering D3.js [Video]

ISBN: 978-1-78398-578-4   Duration: 02:42 hours

Master the art of creating interesting and effective data visualizations with D3.js

1. Watch a real data visualization grow from nothing to something awesome right before your eyes.

2. Scrape data from the web and learn to process it effectively to build a great app.

3. Master D3.js with real-world code samples, tips and tricks, and hard-earned lessons about clean code.

Data Visualization with D3 and AngularJS

ISBN: 978-1-78439-848-4   Paperback: 278 pages

Build dynamic and interactive visualizations from real-world data with D3 on AngularJS

1. Explore the powerful vector graphics capabilities of modern browsers to build customized cross-platform visualizations using D3.js's data-driven techniques.

2. Learn how to modularize a visualization into reusable and testable components using the powerful concepts of modern web application design with AngularJS.

Please check **www.PacktPub.com** for information on our titles